Tales from the Camino

Camino

*Getting Lost and Found on the
Ancient Way of St. James*

MICHAEL HURLEY

RAGBAGGER PRESS

CHARLESTON

Library of Congress Control Number: 2016954047

Hurley, Michael C., 1958-
Tales from the Camino
Michael Hurley
ISBN: 0-9961901-4-7
ISBN-13: 978-0-9961901-4-5
1. Spirituality 2. Travel 3. Relationships I. Title

Printed in the United States of America

1 3 5 7 9 10 8 6 4 2

First Edition: December 1, 2016

For Jillian

"Do not neglect to show kindness to strangers, for thereby some have entertained angels unawares."

THE BOOK OF HEBREWS

CONTENTS

ABOUT THIS BOOK

In July 2015, at the age of fifty-seven, I found myself in an utterly unexpected place in life. As explained in more detail in the Foreword, my odyssey began in Charleston, South Carolina with the loss of my marriage and the sale of virtually everything I owned. I traveled the following month to Europe where, quite coincidentally (or, as it seemed more likely in hindsight, providentially), my feet found their way onto the ancient pilgrim way known as the Camino de Santiago de Compostela. Reeling from these dramatic changes and starved for connection, I took time each day to write short reports of my experiences and epiphanies to a few friends and family. These posts, ranging in length and character from scattered musings to deep meditations, ran nearly 20,000 words by the end of my journey two months later.

All the original posts from my journey have been collected into *Tales from the Camino*, edited lightly for accuracy and relevance. Some are little more than quick notes, while others are long epistles, but all were intended to convey something of the wondrous strangeness I was experiencing. I have seen fit to publish them as historical markers of my life. Inasmuch as providence has seen some purpose in bringing you to these pages, dear reader, I hope they will shed light upon your own path.

FOREWORD

PILGRIM'S PROGRESS

It has been a little more than a year, now. I remember well the day. It was filled with the kind of eruptions seemingly about nothing in particular that, in a marriage, are too often the harbingers of something very particular. Such arguments always seem random and senseless at the time. Only in hindsight do we recognize them as volcanic, arising from deep, unseen fissures that open slowly as a relationship comes apart. They may lie dormant for a while, but eventually they widen and explode. A critical eruption in my life came at ten o'clock in the evening of July 17, 2015, when my wife of five years asked for a divorce. I lacked the will to fight. The truth be told, I felt a strange mixture of fear and relief that she had spoken out loud what we'd both been thinking.

It was not the first time. There had been tremors before. We had separated the previous May, then had a change of heart in June. Now, the pendulum had swung back. I felt a sense of defeat, of inevitability.

Divorce, that always inopportune change of life, happened at an especially inopportune time for me. Six weeks earlier, I had been rescued five hundred miles south of Nova Scotia in the Atlantic Ocean after my thirty-foot sloop started taking on water from structural damage. Offered rescue by a passing ship, I made the decision to abandon my boat and my quest to sail solo to Ireland, where my wife and I had planned to reunite and, however naïvely, renew our vows. A week later I returned to Charleston amid some modest fanfare from an AP story about the rescue, but deep down I was still adrift. I was embarrassed about how the voyage had ended. I felt a little foolish and more than a little sad. I had failed. Six months earlier, the world had looked much brighter.

On January 1, 2015, I had sold my North Carolina law practice to a large firm, found a home for my employees, and, at the age of fifty-six, walked away from a satisfying, thirty-year career as a trial lawyer. I wasn't rich, but I was excited and animated by the new possibilities for my life, which is a feeling money can't buy. My wife had taken a big job for a six-figure salary in her home town and moved back ahead of me to the lovely house where she had lived before we married. Selling my practice in Raleigh made it possible for me to join her. My children were out of college, away from home, and happily employed. I felt the pressure of professional life and the burden of being the primary breadwinner subside for the first time in three decades. I had high hopes for a more fulfilling future as a part-time novelist and a full-time English teacher. I took and passed my teaching certification exams, but my job-search sputtered. Although I applied to dozens of schools in the spring of 2015, the door to full-time employment remained shut.

The fall semester promised new opportunities for employment in teaching, but in the meantime, I looked forward to my first summer off in forty years. I owned an old sailboat, and the sea beckoned. A solo passage to Ireland offered a grand adventure and some publicity for my third novel, then in progress. The two months I planned to take to complete the voyage would fulfill the sea-time requirement to renew the commercial captain's license I had acquired in 1992—handy, we thought, for a possible future venture running weekend charters. Even better, the marina rates in Ireland were half the cost of berthing a boat in Charleston Harbor. Better still, the savings on slip rent meant we could keep the boat as a second home in Europe and afford romantic getaways as we'd done before in the Bahamas and the Dominican Republic. But all those dreams slipped beneath the waves when *Prodigal* was lost. Six weeks after I returned from that disastrous passage, my marriage had foundered and sunk as well—my *second* marriage, mind you. I was embarrassed. I felt foolish. I had failed—again.

On that night of July 17, the new reality of my life was defined by everything that was missing from it: I had no job, no title, no staff, no office to go to every morning, no reason to put on a smart suit and tie, no clients clamoring for my advice, no house, no home, no boat—and, suddenly, no wife and no plan. There was very little left of the identity I had created for myself over the past forty years. Everything had changed, and so I made a decision to change everything.

Over the course of the next three weeks, I sold all that I owned—that is, whatever I didn't absolutely need that anyone would buy, which was nearly all of it: a car, a truck, a grand piano, a canoe, a pop-up camper, toys and gear and equipment and computers and books and artwork and jewelry and knickknacks of all descriptions. The rest I gave away or left behind. At the same time, I began buying the tools of a pilgrim: a backpack, good boots, a sleeping bag, rain gear. Most importantly, I bought a plane ticket—to Dublin.

With nowhere in particular to go, I decided to go to Ireland, the land of my lately disappointed dreams, and wander awhile. I needed to live frugally, that much was clear, but I wasn't about to surrender to fear over money, slink back to Raleigh, tail tucked between my legs, and resume the practice of law. I was in reasonably good shape, physically. Backpacking across Europe was something I had always regretted not doing after college and had never thereafter had the means or time to do. The liberation and excitement of simplifying my life and embarking on a new adventure obscured, for a time, the sadness of what was prompting those changes. I flew to Ireland on August 11 and set out on the Wicklow Way, a hiking trail through the rolling hills south of Dublin.

The first night, I was caught unawares by a feeling of abject loneliness in the small bivouac I had pitched in an unnamed wood. On the second day, still resolute, I chanced to meet four women who cheered me with stories of the Camino de Santiago de Compostela, the "Way of Saint James," an ancient footpath travelled by pilgrims for a thousand years to the shrine of the apostle in Spain. If I ever wanted to go, they explained, I needed only to take a cheap flight from Dublin to Biarritz, and from there a train to St. Jean Pied de Port, in France, where the pilgrimage begins. They wished me well and left me alone again with my thoughts. By the morning of the third day, despair had set in along with the stark reality that I had lost much of what I had once known as "my life." I was overwhelmed.

Starved for sleep, I found myself literally without the physical strength to climb the modest hill that loomed before me. I turned back, found a bed and breakfast with an Internet connection, and hastily wrote an email to my wife with a subject line that read, "Please Take Me Back." I also wrote to friends, whom I had left with the glib and false impression that I was happily resolved to return to the single life, and admitted that I felt very much at the end of my rope. I needed rescue, but rescue came in an unexpected form. My wife answered my plea with a simple but firm refusal. In the end it would be her greatest gift to me: the gift of finality and clarity from which come healing and acceptance. There was no going back, this time. The only way left to me was the way forward. It was then I vaguely recalled the sparse details of my conversation with the four women. Over the next twenty-four hours, I winnowed my possessions further—some thirty pounds' worth. My bed-and-breakfast hosts became the startled recipients of various items of camping gear I wouldn't need or couldn't bear to carry on the 530 miles of the Camino. I shipped a laptop and cameras and cables and hard drives back to friends in the USA and boarded a plane. I had no guidebook. In fact, I barely knew where or what the Camino was. I relied heavily on the vague advice that all would be clear once I arrived in St. Jean. It was not.

The people at the help desk in the Biarritz airport spoke only French, not English or Spanish. Through a series of pantomimes, a pleasant woman explained that I was to walk outside to the curb and wait for the bus to Bayonne.

In Bayonne I had my first meal in a French café, then more pantomimes with other pleasant people revealed that I was to take a second bus from there to St. Jean. By then I had joined a small knot of anxious pilgrims, all making our way for the first time to the same strange place. The volunteers staffing the tiny office set up in St. Jean spoke very little English but could not have been more caring. When it became clear that every albergue (hostel) in the village was full, they led me and twenty other late-arrivers to a gymnasium to spend the night in our sleeping bags on wrestling mats.

On the first morning of the Camino, I lacked a key bit of information. I had no idea which way to go. I learned then the most valuable lessons of life as a pilgrim: *humility* and *patience*. I didn't know everything anymore. In fact, I didn't know much of anything. I was *dependent* on others. I needed their help, and I needed to be willing to wait for it. I had to follow and trust people other than myself. And I did.

Through the happenstance and serendipity by which friendships are so often made on the Camino, I made new friends every day. We shared directions, advice, bandages, hopes, fears, sorrows, and stories. For so little money, I enjoyed simple and delicious meals and good wine. I savored, even more than the tapas, long hours of conversation with pilgrims from Australia, Malaysia, Germany, England, Ireland, Spain, Belgium, Russia, Norway, Poland, Italy, Denmark, France, Argentina, Brazil, South Africa, Slovakia, and a dozen other countries I can't remember.

Through it all, for two months and five hundred miles, I steadfastly refused to read a guidebook. Each day, I had no idea what lay ahead, how far I would go, when the next albergue would appear, or where I would find an open bed for the night. I simply walked and followed my fellow pilgrims. When I was thirsty, a village fountain would eventually appear, flowing with cool, clear water. When I was hungry, I would pass a café around a corner in a tiny village, its cases filled with food and its taps glistening with sweat from ice-cold San Miguel beer. New people and places and experiences and insights came to me when they were most needed, as if by the mystery of providence, every day. The Camino changed my life, and when I finally saw the giant botafumeiro soaring through the corridors of the cathedral in Santiago, my life changed again. Having failed at so much of late, I felt astonishing success when I reached the ocean at Finisterre. But my progress as a pilgrim didn't end there.

I was still on the Camino when I formed the plan come to Great Britain after I finished. I wanted a quiet place to hunker down for the winter and finish writing *The Passage*, which had been put on hold with all that followed the decision to divorce. A cottage on those lush, mist-soaked hills of Wales seemed the best, and importantly, most affordable choice. It was a brilliant choice at that. It rained every day in the little town of Machynlleth (pronounced "Mack-HUNK-leth" by the Welsh), forcing me to sit indoors and write. I was also befriended and encouraged by my landlord's two cats, who sat on my desk while I toiled over my work, scowling disapproval whenever I left to warm myself by the wood stove, make another cup of the ubiquitous tea with milk, or fry up a bit of sausage and mash. When the clouds parted, I would dash out for a four-mile walk along the river into town in my newly acquired Wellie boots and wax coat—the essential livery of all Welsh travelers. Such shades of green as there are in the countryside of Wales I have seen nowhere else but the Emerald Isle, which shares much the same climate.

While my words marched across the page, time marched on as well. I felt a tinge of uneasiness born of the impermanence of my situation. As much as I enjoyed life as a lodger in other people's homes, it hardly seemed a good arrangement for the long term. Moreover, I remained in Great Britain only at the pleasure of the government, which had given me a maximum of six months to enjoy the privilege. Although my grandfather was born in London in 1878, this afforded me, as an American, no special right to remain in the country of his birth. I had to get out by April 12, 2016, per the warning clearly stamped on my passport. I needed a plan. Once again I looked to the sea.

A well-found cruising sailboat is a many-splendored thing: a magic carpet, a snug and safe home in all weathers, a marvel of engineering, a figment of romance, a bearer of dreams. I should know. I have loved many of them and lost two of them at sea. Acquiring a third seemed to tempt fate, but I had safely called fate's bluff when I left America. I knew the sailing life as well as I knew any life outside a courtroom. I warmed to the idea of another boat, but it would have to be a modest vessel at a modest price. There are many such boats, forgotten and unloved, with good bones and strong hearts, languishing in the marinas of the world. It was just a matter of finding the right one.

My search for the particular magic carpet that would carry me away started in November 2015 and took me along Britain's remarkable railway system to Plymouth, on the southern coast, Walton-on-Naze, in the East, and Pwllheli (pronounced "Pull-HELLY") in northern Wales. But these travels revealed no suitable vessel for my adventure. I despaired of the sailing plan altogether and considered finding new lodging for the spring and summer elsewhere, but before long an old British-built boat—one of the famed Nicholson 32s by Camper-Nicholson–caught my eye. There reportedly are more people who have flown in outer space than have circumnavigated in small sailboats, but no fewer than eight Nicholson 32s have circled the globe. The great number of them still available on the used boat market in Britain and elsewhere is testament to their sound construction.

I moved from Wales to London in January, continued to toil away at *The Passage,* and in February purchased the 1967 Nicholson 32 that I renamed *Nevermore,* borrowing from Poe's famous poem, *The Raven.* My reasons were not as macabre as Poe's. The name for me signified that this was my last chance. There would never be another boat, another time, or another hope for the sailing adventure of my dreams. She would not only be my home. I resolved to take her around the world. When all was ready, I sailed into the English Channel at Calais, bound for the Canary Islands.

The passage to the island of La Palma spanned eighteen days and a total of 2,215 miles for an average speed of a little more than five miles per hour—my longest and most successful nonstop ocean passage to-date. Most of that time was spent hundreds of miles out to sea, but for two days a southwest gale forced me close to the northwestern tip of Spain. I sailed within twenty miles of the cliffs of Finisterre, where I had finished the Camino seven months earlier and sat wondering where life might take me next. Then, I had never dreamed it would take me once again to sea, much less to the very patch of ocean before my eyes. After the disaster that had befallen *Prodigal* the year before, seeing the volcanic peak of La Palma rise 8,000 feet on the horizon on the morning of May 23, 2016, after eighteen days alone at sea, was not just a thrill. It was a requiem for all that I had lost.

As I write these words, I am enjoying life back in London while *Nevermore* tugs at her dock lines in La Palma. The next passage, 3,100 miles nonstop across the Atlantic to St. Lucia, looms large in my imagination. Hurricane season must pass first, but it *will* pass. If all goes as planned, I will board a plane for La Palma in December, and *Nevermore* will sail again in January. It is already September, but there is yet a little time to savor the past and ponder the vast unknown that has become my future—a pilgrimage to my own dreams. Yet as ethereal as dreams can be, today the ground feels surprisingly firm under my feet.

When I finished the Camino and arrived in Finisterre— a village whose name means literally "the end of the earth"—it seemed I had nowhere else to go. The eruptions that had ended my marriage and thrown my feet upon the Way of St. James had been violent and transformative. As if to underscore the all-too-real fact that I had been pushed to the brink—to the end of my rope, as I described it at the time—I had followed the pilgrim way to that most final of all ending places, where lost souls seeking absolution had for centuries literally chased God into the sea. But as I would come to learn, that place and that time was not the end—not the end of the world, or my life, or of me.

The strange and wonderful truth about volcanoes is that, for all their destructiveness, they are the only things on Earth that can actually create something new under the sun. While climbing the summit in La Palma last June, I heard hikers remark that there are acres of land formed by volcanic eruptions on the island that are only fifty years old. Imagine that. After four billion years, the Earth is still erupting and reinventing itself. Why should we be any different?

In the year since I wept in a nameless wood as a friendless foreigner on Irish soil, much of the chaff in my life has been burned away. All of my clothes now fit in a small carry-on bag, and I still feel like I have too much. Everything else I own, including the boat on which I will live and travel, fits into a thirty-two by nine-foot space. I have developed a visceral aversion to shopping and the acquisition of "things." I want for nothing—not because I have so much, but because the things I value are so few and mostly free. I earn a pittance from my novels, but I owe no one a dime. Yet for all I have lost, whole new vistas have appeared as if by magic before my eyes.

There are people in countries all over the world— fellow pilgrims I met along the Way of St. James—who know my name and share a special part of my memories, who wish me well and carry my good will in return. They follow my progress through life as I follow theirs. There are people here in London and all across England and Wales who think of me, worry about me, love and care for me. These are souls who were unknown to me and I to them before the eruptions in my life cast me out into the void. They softened my fall. They are as new soil under my feet, the firm ground upon which I travel.

"Leap," John Burroughs wrote, "and the net will appear." How very true. If only we could so believe, what a solid footing, and a loving embrace, we would find.

CHAPTER ONE

THE WAY

August 17

Attended my first Catholic mass in years tonight in Roncesvalles. There were pilgrims from all parts of the globe. I was promptly recruited to do the English readings as "el hombre de Sur Carolina." I have a hard time following the lispy dialect they speak in Spain, but I remember the liturgy. When they said, "Lord, I am not worthy to receive you, but only say the word and I shall be healed," it made me weep.

August 18

Feeling stronger every day. I hit the trail today and went like a train, faster after fifteen miles than when I started. Another few days of this and I'll be ready to take the midfield against Hopkins. The tapas are to die for, and so cheap. In Zubiri for the night. Thinking of spending the winter in Seville. The walking is such wonderful therapy. I love this country, and my Spanish is improving. I am a total Boomer cliché, listening to James Taylor on my headphones as I go. Thank God for the Camino. It is saving my life.

August 19

All settled in magnificent Pamplona after a long walk from Zubiri. Room in a very modern albergue right on the Camino in the heart of the old city, €14 a night, including hot shower and breakfast. I am meeting new people from all over the world and getting lots of advice on what to do with my life. There is a great camaraderie among the peregrinos (pilgrims). Headed out shortly in search of tapas and wine.

August 20

A long, hot walk from Pamplona to Puente La Reina today, about sixteen miles. A deluxe hotel room for €10 makes it all the sweeter, though. The weather has been spectacular. I love talking to the locals. They are so friendly. One of a group of women from Barcelona needed moleskin and scissors for blisters, and I happened to have both in my pack, earning me the name "Miguel mi Salvador y el Angel de Sur Carolina." All in a day's work. My own feet are holding up well so far. I'm thoroughly beat by the end of the day, but ready to go in the morning. Little blessings appear when you need them most, like a delicious cured ham, cheese, tomato and olive oil sandwich and ice cold San Miguel cerveza in Zariquiegue. Stopped at the church there and lit a candle for an old friend recently diagnosed with breast cancer, to whom I dedicated my Camino from the start. All is mostly well with me. I have no complaints.

August 21

Greetings from Estella. Another bluebird day on a hot, dusty trail, fifteen miles through vineyards and olive groves, and I am beginning to think I am the luckiest man alive. I was so worn out and beaten down by the Spanish sun today that when Stevie Ray Vaughn's version of "Little Wing" came on my headphones around two o'clock, I almost had an out-of-body experience. I am staying in a very modern hostel attached to a 17th century church. Every place I have been in Spain is immaculate. The people who run the hostels or albergues are not just unfailingly patient and polite; they have treated me with the utmost respect bordering on reverence for the sacred status of a pilgrim. So mystical is the power of this journey that even the elderly priest in Roncesvalles asked us to pray for him when we reach Compostela. Like most pilgrims on the way I have my doubts, but without doubt there can be no faith. My faith is in the Nazarene who died, was buried, and on the third day rose again, appearing to thousands who told the Good News that we still tell today. ¡Buen Camino!

August 22

A lovely walk from Estella to Los Arcos that began in the early morning hours, joined by my new friend Nathalie, a forty-six-year old massage therapist and yoga instructor from Barcelona. She speaks no English, but on our long walk together I learned that she is the seventh of nine children of a French mother from Alsace who plays the piano and a Spanish father from Catalan who plays the violin; that she likes white wine with fish and red wine with cheese but prefers white; and that "el secreto de la vida" (the secret of life) is to go with the flow, take what comes, and not sweat the small stuff. She is headed back to Barcelona now. I meet very few people who are walking the entire Camino and feel very fortunate to have that chance. I have also met Jeff and Anna, two British ex-pats who have lots of advice for me, including that I spend the winter living and writing a bestseller in Yorkshire. Considering all of the above as I rest my weary feet and dream of tonight's tapas . . .

August 24

So, the journey goes on. A long hard slog of twenty-four miles from Viana to Najera today, with a full pack. My feet are on fire. The pilgrim ranks are thinning out. Just two young men from Belgium in the albergue tonight. My friends Sylvia and Yolanda from Valencia walked part of the way with me before catching a bus home. It's hard not to smile and laugh on the Camino, but when I told them over lunch that I was deeply sad to be going through a divorce, they were surprised for two reasons. First, apparently sadness for a lost love is something no man in Spain would ever admit to, and secondly, their impression of Americans is that we are all quite literally fat and happy, and I seemed to be neither. In any event, after hearing this they and the bar owner steadfastly refused to let me pay for my drinks and meal, and they sent me off with great hugs and well-wishes for a buen Camino. Everyone over forty on this journey is going through some sort of crisis, and everyone under forty is going for the adventure. As for me, I am just going day by day and taking life as it comes. It's a lonely road much of the time, but I love hearing from all of you, so please stay in touch.

August 25

A short day of just 10.5 miles. I am nursing a bad blister on the little toe of my right foot that has expanded to remove the nail and surrounding skin. I don't want to gross anyone out, but I have attached a photo in hopes that my medical friends might see it and share some treatment advice. It looks worse than it feels. It doesn't hurt at all except when I walk, and after fifty yards or so my mind starts ignoring the pain and I can walk almost normally until I stop and the pain returns. I am cleaning with alcohol pads and packing in gauze with Neosporin. I am not stopping, nor am I complaining. I wouldn't dare. In the albergue with us tonight is a seventy-eight-year-old woman who can barely walk. She has come the same distance I have traveled.

Otherwise . . . it's just another day in Paradise. I have stopped for the night at the Albergue de La Virgen de Guadalupe in the tiny town of Ciruena, population twenty people and two dogs. Pedro Marie is preparing dinner and breakfast, which with the bed and shower runs €13, total. There is a Puerto Rican man in the bunk next to mine who shares my lament that the drink maví, sold in Old San Juan, can be found nowhere else. There are two young girls and a young man from Denmark and a young man from Japan with us. I am the lone American almost everywhere I go. We all are nursing blistered feet.

I am lagging six kilometers behind two fleet-footed

British friends, Anna and Jeff, who have taken a considered interest in my welfare in view of my general divorce malaise. To cheer me up they have engaged in unprovoked speculation about who "the perfect wife" might be, all of which I have disregarded on the premise that there is no such thing. When pressed, I suggested a prim Anglican church secretary who loves books and music and is filled with secret longing, which Anna promptly shot down with this reply: "Good God, man, don't you read vintage British crime fiction? Such types are generally responsible for murder most foul!" So it seems I am doomed, whatever comes.

Speaking of Britain, I overlooked the fact that by the time I hobble into Finisterre, I will have used up my ninety-day visa in Spain and, like a boll weevil, will have to fly off somewhere else in search of a home. So, Seville for the winter won't be possible. France is too expensive, and the language is a definite barrier. Everywhere else is too cold, so it's looking like I'll spend November, December and January in the UK where thru Airbnb.com a wandering bachelor can rent a room in a nice country home for a fourth of what it would cost to rent an utterly depressing apartment in the worst part of Charleston. The city fathers in Charleston are busy fining anyone who tries to rent out a room without a hotel license, while in Europe Airbnb.com is blooming, aiding the local economy, and making overseas travel more affordable.

Over the winter in the UK I will finish my current novel, *The Passage*. Because my grandfather was born in London, I may qualify for a longer visa in England, I am told. If so, I may stay there through the spring and summer to complete two more books. If not, I may come back to Spain to find a room, begin another ninety-day stint, and continue writing, etc., before returning to the U.S. in fall 2016 to begin some form of honest labor. I am not the least bit homesick. Not having a home or a life to return to has proven to be the perfect vaccine for that illness. However, the Camino is the only cure for the profound sense of failure I feel, and I am taking my treatments daily.

That, for the moment, is the plan. My heartfelt thanks to all for your prayers and encouragement. I am doing my best to find my way. The mystical journey continues tomorrow . . .

August 26

18.66 long, hot miles got me to Belogrado, today. With man this is not possible, but with Tylenol Extra Strength 500 mg., all things are possible.

Met a young fellow from Belgium on the way, today. He is on the Camino to get over a two-year relationship with a best friend's twenty-year-old little sister, whom he met during tango lessons. She loves him more than life itself, he tells me, but she is driving him crazy with her neediness. She's in college. He dropped out and isn't sure what he wants to do—hence the Camino. I told him not to worry, that his twenty-year-old girlfriend was likely getting less needy by the minute and would soon replace him with head-spinning alacrity. He doubted this as only a twenty-three-year-old could. His knees also gave out on him two weeks ago in the Pyrenees, so he lagged behind, and we were soon parted. I went on my way, feeling like a healthy sage of fifty-seven.

I am holding my own so far. In a small miracle for which the Camino is duly famous, when I thought I could go no farther today, the three things I needed most in this world—a bar, a pharmacy, and an ATM, all appeared within twenty yards of the same corner in a little village at the top of a high, hot, dusty hill. I stocked up on Tylenol, bandages, Betadyne cream, tape, and moleskin.

My Belgian friend told me that none of his friends is married, and those that do marry have no more than one child. "So Belgium is disappearing, then?" I asked. "No," he told me. The country is filling up with immigrants from Turkey, Morocco, and Syria, he explained, who are not assimilating into the local culture. This is the story I hear from people all over Europe. There is a sense of crisis for the disappearance of national identity, but no one knows the solution.

I passed an ancient church on the Camino, today, with some impressive, ancient statuary. Amid all the antiquity was a coin-operated electronic-candle prayer-altar. Instead of putting a coin in the poor-box voluntarily and lighting a real candle, you drop your money in the machine and one little bulb lights up to lift your prayers to God. Only the Catholic Church could do this without blushing, but who am I to begrudge the Almighty a few coins? I paid the money and said my prayers.

August 27

Taking a layover day in Belogrado to give my legs a rest and heal up a bit. Off in the morning to the next village. In the meantime, I have been doing a bit more research on where I might land after the Camino. There is a nice

arrangement available for the winte:
Machynlleth, Wales. Seems like the
needing several uninterrupted n
comments and advice.

August 28

A modest 9.36 miles today brought me to the
fabulously renovated 14th century pilgrim hostel in
Villafranca Montes de Oca, which could be a Hilton
except for the price of €5 a night. My stocking feet feel
great padding around on the marble floors in the lobby, so
I think the boots may be the issue. I plan to buy a good
pair of sandals at the first opportunity.

With my layover day, the old Danish nurse I met two
days earlier who has suffered a stroke and walks with a
slow, uneven gait, was briefly ahead of me. I am in awe of
her. She speaks little English, and I speak no Danish, so
we exchange only a brief "hah-low," but she is a living
testament to the power of this journey. It is deeply,
profoundly meaningful to many. This woman is not here
for the exercise. She is suffering every day.

About the Camino . . . It goes back more than 1,000
years to the Middle Ages, when even more people made
the five-hundred mile trip than do today, owing to the
special indulgence granted by the church to pilgrims who
completed it. Many of the villages I am passing grew up to
serve the pilgrims on the way. Tradition holds that
sometime in the 10th century, a hermit followed a star
shining on a field where he found the buried remains of
the Apostle James, beheaded in Jerusalem hundreds of
years earlier. A shrine, then a church, then a city grew up

site of the discovery, named Santiago (St.
de Compostela (of the field of the star). The
ess ghost of St. James is believed to have appeared
olding a sword while mounted on a horse in the battle
that drove the Moors from Spain. In the ancient church I
passed in Belogrado this morning I found a statue of St.
James, obligingly holding his own head.

There is substantial reason if not overwhelming
evidence to refute the claim that the actual remains of
James, the brother of Jesus, are anywhere in Spain much
less Compostela. But once on the Camino, you have joined
the church of those many millions of saints and sinners,
including Francis of Assisi, who for centuries have made
this exact journey in search of answers that lie beyond the
world of reason and evidence. I am seeking a few answers
of my own. The walk for me is at once so deeply sad and
greatly joyous, so terribly lonely and wonderfully hopeful.

There are many, of course, for whom the Camino is
entirely about speed, time and distance, and these seem to
be primarily Latino men whizzing by on bikes. They have
passed me by the hundreds, all wearing brightly colored,
extremely tight-fitting Lycra racing suits, all intensely
machismo, and all pumping hard. I have not seen a single
dude lollygagging by on a Schwinn wearing Dockers and
Topsiders with his shirt tail flapping in the breeze. They do
not exist in Spain. The "muy macho" image of the Latino
male is not a forgotten stereotype of *I Love Lucy* reruns. It
is alive and well. To a greater or lesser degree, most
Spanish men seem to me to exhibit a sense of bravado,
formality, and dignity. Hemingway didn't make this stuff
up; he just wrote it down. A few days ago I sat in a bar full
of men and women watching a TV in silent, rapt attention

as a bullfighter wearing a bucket of Brylcreem in his hair and pants two sizes too small strutted his way around a terrified animal slowly dying from blood loss. I don't know if this is what Spanish women want, but it must be, because they are getting it in spades. Alan Alda couldn't get a date here to save his life. . . . Which of course means I am exactly where I need to be.

August 29

11.33 nearly painless miles today to the tiny village of Agés. I ditched the boots in favor of a pair of Sanuk-brand sandals and felt great. Should be ready for a longer trek tomorrow.

Met people today from Italy, Korea, Holland and Canada, and sharing a dorm room tonight with two sisters from Poland who speak almost no English. I have an app from Google on my smartphone that translates spoken conversation, and they are delighted with it. One told me this is the first time she has been able to have a conversation with an American.

No other Yanks anywhere, as usual. Everyone who hears I'm from the states assumes I live in New York City. No one knows where South Carolina is.

The dorm is a small room with six bunk beds above a restaurant and bar. Headed downstairs in a minute with my Kindle for a cold Estrella. I'm reading Hemingway's *For Whom The Bell Tolls* and Diarmid McCullough's *History of Christianity*. Enjoying this more relaxed pace.

August 30

Greetings from Burgos! 15.59 miles today took us through the mystical hills outside Atapuerca, where after a long and winding climb up a rocky trail we came to a tall wooden cross amid a pile of stones. This is the not the particular iron cross site filmed in the Martin Sheen movie, *The Way*. That one, the venerated "Cruz de Ferro," lies farther ahead.

August 31

Spent a layover day here in Burgos to explore this city's remarkable cathedral, founded in 1210, which houses an endless museum of art, statuary, and artifacts accumulated over nine centuries. The cathedral itself is an architectural marvel and absolutely huge. Photography is discouraged. The cathedral houses some dozen chapels each about the size of Grace Church in Charleston or Christ Church in Raleigh. You could spend a week here and not fully appreciate it all.

Back on the road again, tomorrow. Blister situation stable. Am amazed at the number of young people I meet who are unable to continue because they've been racing to finish within a month and pushing themselves too hard each day. I remain a committed lollygagger content to get there when I get there.

All is well with me. Love hearing from everyone. You're so kind to cheer me on.

September 1

Greetings from Hornillos del Camino. I started walking at 5:30 this morning from Burgos to cover 13.7 miles in about six hours. Stopped along the way for breakfast of pincho de tortilla (potato quiche), cafe con leche (sweet coffee with milk), and baguettes in a tiny village at a tiny bar at which two tiny dogs and I were the only customers.

The bartender complimented my Spanish. I don't speak especially well, but locals are always so astonished and grateful to hear an American speak any Spanish at all. They invariably ask me where I learned the language. I tell them in Puerto Rico in 1972, where once at the dinner table of my uncle Jose and Aunts Carmelina and Angelina I made the mistake of saying Spanish was more confusing to learn than English and received a withering rebuttal.

The bartender said that it was nice to see an American who was "muy tranquilo" (very relaxed) because Americans are always in such a hurry on the Camino. (So much for my earlier stereotyping of Latino men.) This seemed foolish to him, he said, because "el Camino no se va" (the road isn't going anywhere). He then reached into his pocket, pulled out a medal, and gave it to me with a wish for a "buen Camino." The medal bears the image of Mary and is inscribed in Spanish with these words: "Oh Mary, conceived without sin, pray for us who have recourse to you."

The world of the Camino seems to swirl like the wind with little moments of grace like these. I have deliberately refused to carry a map or a guidebook in order to force myself to interact with others and encounter these gifts of grace. Whenever I am uncertain where to go, if there are

no other pilgrims ahead to follow, I have only to ask a local, "El Camino pasa por aqui?" (Does the Camino pass by here?") to receive the most enthusiastic and demonstrative instructions. It doesn't matter how old or young they are, absolutely everyone knows where the Camino goes. More than once when I have missed a turn, I have heard someone whistle or shout "peregrino" (pilgrim) and turned around to see them pointing me in the right direction.

What I love about Spain is not only that they have delicious wine that is dirt cheap, but that they are so much less fussy about the whole matter than the French. There is no Cabernet or Bordeaux or Chardonnay or Sauvignon Blanc. There is only tinto (red) or blanco (white) for 3€ a bottle.

September 2

Fourteen miles took me to Castrojirez, today. All is well. I am at a hippie albergue swirling with incense that looks something like a well-worn frat house in Haight Ashbury, but it is clean, and the people are friendly as always.

The Camino is a communal experience, especially in the small villages, and you find any available seat in a restaurant. Last night, I ate delicious seafood paella seated next to an elderly, retired school teacher from Quebec. She hates the cold weather but cannot bear to leave Canada, and she is finding her own way following a thirty-five year marriage that ended unexpectedly in divorce five years ago. She had to be treated in a hospital along the way for bug bites. ("Imagine that," she said, "a Canadian complaining

about bug bites.") She cannot see well, and as a result has gotten lost a few times. And yet, she was as cheerful and eager for the journey as anyone I've met. So, needless to say, I have completely stopped feeling the least bit sorry for myself or complaining to anyone.

I have been getting up well before dawn and walking in the cool darkness for the first five miles or so. Winter was in the air today. One man passed me wearing ski gloves. The Camino has become my daily meditation and vocation. I shall miss it, but thankfully not any time soon, as I am not yet even half the way to Santiago.

I had dinner tonight with a grandmother from France. She spoke no English. I was so utterly at a loss that I could do no more than sing the songs taught to me as a child by my big sister Suzanne Hurley, "Frere Jacques" and "Alloutte, Gentile Alloutte," followed by a mindless recitation of the French celebrities whose names I blurted out randomly, beginning and ending with Catherine Denouve and Brigit Bardot. We had a lovely dinner, but I'm sure she thinks I am a nostalgically lecherous imbecile. Fluency in languages is the universal passport in Europe. How I wish I knew more. However, I redeemed myself with a flawless solo performance of the American national anthem on a dare by two Irish girls in our suite, which earned me a polite smattering of applause from around the albergue. God Bless America, the land that I love.

September 3

17.3 miles fetched Fromista this afternoon. All is well. I am roughly at mile 230 of the 500 mile journey from St. Jean Pied de Port to Santiago de Compostela. Today was a

blustery, cool day walking over steep hills and long, dry plains. I am lost in thought most of the time. Jeff Trueman, a British expat and one of several fine friends I have met on the Camino, has refused to let me mope or take my troubles too seriously. In that vein today he sent a link to two great WWI marching tunes to help lift me out of my doldrums. There's something to this stiff upper lip business about the English. It is indeed "a long way to Tipperary" (and Santiago), but if I "pack up my troubles in my old kit bag," I shall be there, and in a far better place, before long.

September 4

"You know you're old, don't you?" Someone said this to me a few months ago when I announced "Plan B" (walking across a good piece of Spain) after "Plan A" (for better or worse, for richer or poorer) had come to grief. Old is one thing, but old and unwanted is what you drop off at the Goodwill store. I wasn't ready for the rag bag, so I grabbed a backpack and flew to Europe.

It's true, I am old—fifty-seven years old, to be exact— and I was feeling every day of it this morning when I decided to sleep late in the albergue in Fromista. Sleeping is something old folks do a lot of. I knew this was annoying the young up-and-at-em Germans in my dorm room. The boy flipped the switch for the overhead light in the predawn darkness to get ready, and I heard his girlfriend scold him. The light abruptly switched off. I don't speak German, but judging from her clipped elocution and the timing of the light, I'm sure it was something about not wanting to wake the elderly

American still sleeping in the last bunk. In a mixture of guilt and embarrassment, I rolled out of bed and started my day.

My feet still ached from yesterday's seventeen miles, and I had a blister the size of Nebraska forming on the ball of my left foot. Just two miles in, today, I had already stopped to savor my second cup of cafe Americano and was wondering how bad it would look if I stopped for the night well short of the thirteen miles to my next destination. Then something wonderful happened.

I got a text message from Nathalie, the young woman I had first met on the Camino coming out of Pamplona, two weeks ago. Back then she was walking ahead of me, and I especially noticed two things about her. One was her clothing. Every day on the Camino I look the same——like I've spent the last two weeks shooting an episode of *Mutual of Omaha's Wild Kingdom* in a dust storm——but she looked fresh and clean and relaxed and hip and cool. She was bouncing down the Camino in airy, Moorish style pantaloons that gathered at the ankle. Stylish girl, I thought. The other thing was her hair. It was long and sandy blonde, and it was swaying behind from one shoulder to the other as she walked. I watched it like a metronome until she was out of sight——which, sadly given the difference in our pace, wasn't that long. Pretty girl, I thought.

I saw her off and on that day as we caught up or passed each other at several rest stops along the Camino. By then she was wearing shorts, and I told her I remembered her by her hair and her pants, which I'm sure sounded as strange in Spanish as it does in English.

It was two days later when I saw her again at a food

truck parked along the Camino several miles outside Los Arcos. The Camino has a way of breaking down barriers quickly, and by then we were old friends. She sat down next to me complaining of a sore leg. I offered what could pass for a massage sitting in a plastic chair by the side of a dirt road at noon. We later got up and walked the rest of the day together——now at the same pace, because she was limping. Before long she was leaning on my arm. Poor girl, I thought. When we got to the end, she gave me a hug and caught a bus out of town for the way home.

I cannot tell you my delight today when I read a text message from this young woman, inviting me to spend a few days at her home near the Mediterranean in October, after I finish the Camino. Lucky boy, I thought. I immediately swallowed my second cup of cafe Americano and charged down the path, passing the young Germans as if they were standing still. I'm feeling younger by the minute. ·

PHOTOGRAPHS

(All photos by the author. An index of captions begins on p. 119.)

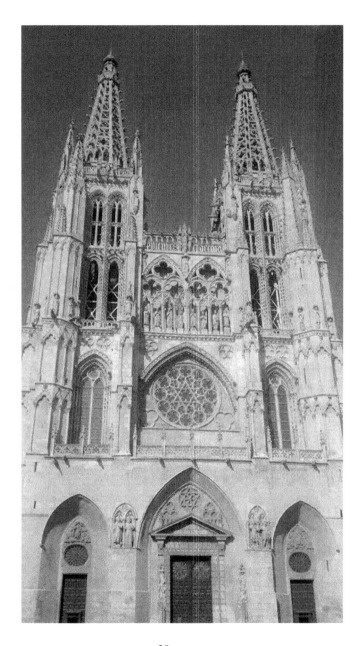

September 5

Greetings and salutations from Ledigos, Spain, the unofficial half-way point of my trek that began in France on August 16, which is as good an occasion as any to wax poetic about the journey. I walked fifteen miles today from Carrion, where I spent the night in the albergue Espiritu Santo, run by the Society of St. Vincent de Paul, of which I was once a member in my holier days. In Carrion, the church treated us to a free concert of classical guitar inside the nave, and it was magical. Spain is the Nashville of classical guitar, and the young artist we heard was well trained.

Today, I walked with no problems with new music headphones plugged in. "Go Ask Alice" by Jefferson Airplane is actually a pretty good marching tune, and I'll bet I was the only man in Spain singing along with George Jones to "He Stopped Loving Her Today." Bob Dylan took the words out of my mouth with "Don't Think Twice, Babe, It's Alright," and I decided to take Steven Still's advice that "If You Can't Be With The One You Love, Love The One You're With."

All is well with me. I am healthy and enjoying the wine, the tapas, the people and the journey. I am gradually getting over my melancholy. As Dylan said, "So long honey babe. Where I'm bound, I can't tell." I have malice toward none and good will toward all. I have absolutely no idea what I'm doing or where I'm going, and for the first time in my life, none of that seems to matter.

September 6

Greetings from Sahagun. A short eleven miles to today's destination. All is well with feet, heart, hands and soul.

I have to tell you, when it comes to the mysticism of the Catholic church, I fall squarely on the side of the doubters and the skeptics. But . . . there is something truly weird if not wonderful about this Camino. Little things keep happening. Things appear that should never appear, and just when I need them. I'll find myself wishing for something, and there it will be. What I need is being supplied. They are little things, yet so utterly improbable and so personal that I dare not describe them. They are precious to me.

It's not just the physical or tangible stuff. There is some sort of aura around this road, and it pushes you along. Sometimes it feels as if I'm walking in a dream. There are whole sections of time that I cannot recall. And then there are the people. Some of them look at me as if they know me—and have known me, a long, long time. Everyone genuinely wishes me well. Every. Single. Person.

And so . . . today when I passed a small, crudely drawn sign lying in the dirt that said "Iglesia Abierto," with an arrow pointing to the left, the literal translation may have been "church open," but what I read was "Michael Hurley, please call home." I turned immediately, of course, as if my feet were on rails.

Every little town in Spain is situated around a church. A Catholic church. The places are lovingly cared for by clusters of old women who show a level of devotion that is humbling to behold. The village church is their center.

This is their core.

After I turned in obedience to the sign, I noticed an elderly man standing alone. Judging from his forlorn expression at the other pilgrims who were passing without even a sidelong glance, I gathered he had drawn the sign imploring them to come. But his face gladdened when he saw me, and in the hope that I might be following the sign, he began slowly to move toward the entrance to the church as I approached.

He welcomed me to a table where he stamped my pilgrim passport in ink with a seal that read "Moratinos, Tierra de Campos," the name of the village. I had planned to stay only briefly to light a candle, but he asked me to attend the mass that was starting in fifteen minutes. I was the only pilgrim there, in a church and a village that probably owed its existence to the Camino. Of course I stayed.

Before long the tiny church filled up, first with old women who fussed over the table linens and candles on the altar, then with what must have been the entire population of the village. To my surprise, the man I saw standing outside, looking forlornly at the passing pilgrims, was the parish priest. He put on his vestments, consecrated the bread and the wine, and fed us the Eucharist.

When mass was over, I said my goodbyes to the woman next to me in the pew. She asked whether I was a pilgrim. When I said yes, she said "pray for us." There was not a soul in that church whose sandal straps I would be worthy to unfasten, and yet their only request was that I pray for them——the second time I have heard that request from a far holier soul. Pray for them I certainly will, and may God help them.

On the subject of prayer, a friend I have known since high school asked me today how she should pray for me. I thought about that question all day, but the best answer didn't occur to me until the song by Miranda Lambert, "Holdin' Onto You" started playing on my phone. Of all the many blessings, gifts, and small miracles the Good Lord has given me, the one he has so far seen fit to withhold is the everlasting love of a woman to have and to hold. I pray one day to find a love like the one Miranda sings about in that beautiful, haunting song. It would take a miracle to find such a love, this late in life. But if a miracle is what I seek, I have come to the best of all possible places.

September 7

At Burgo Ranero after a short twelve-mile hike today. All is well. It is such a joy to be friends with my feet, again. I have no serious issues and am walking well. The Camino is proving to be therapeutic for the aches and pains that earlier plagued me. I have very little swelling or pain. So, if you're looking for a cure-all, I can highly recommend walking five hundred miles through France and Spain.

Not much to show in the way of photos, today. This section was rather drab. I saw the word "empanada" at a cafe for the first time (they were big in Texas in the eighties), so I ordered one and took a photo. Quite good. I thought I'd also show you the typical "pilgrim menu," served at restaurants all along the Camino for about $11 US. It includes a full bottle of wine, a bottle of mineral water, a first course (I choose spaghetti for the extra carbs), a main course (tonight was veal and French fries), and flan or cheesecake or ice cream or fruit for dessert. Try finding that menu in Charleston for eleven bucks.

The albergue here offers beds at no charge for a suggested donation, only. Quite clean, with hot showers and clean bathrooms. The young girl who checked me in asked if she could try out my pack, which she described as "old school." It's true—I'm the only one carrying an external frame pack identical to the one I had as a boy scout in 1969. All the cool kids carry the new fangled internal frame packs that don't let you shift the weight to your hips as well. They can have 'em. I love mine. I told the girl that I am the living incarnation of "old school," and that it was only fitting I should carry a pack to match.

I had to smile today at some one-word graffiti I saw scrawled on a park bench: "podemos." I didn't get it at first, and then the loose translation came to me: "Yes, We Can." Not many Republicans in Spain.

Finally, even here on the Camino the news of the terrible refugee crisis in Europe is ever present. The pope is right: we need to take them in. The reason is simple. I read it written on the wall of some sort of Zen Buddhist hostel in Castrojirez a few days ago. Loosely quoted, it said: "Our greatest delusion in this life is the belief that I am here and you are there." In other words, there is no "them." There is only "us," and we're all in this together. Peace be with you.

September 8

12.35 miles to Mansilla, today. All is well. I started walking to Joe Cocker's "I Get By With A Little Help

From My Friends," thought of Joe, who died this year, and thought of all of you. I have made many new friends here in Spain, as well, and you are all a great gift to me. There are times when I feel as if I'm tightrope walking without a net. Every once in a while I'll "look down" and realize that I have sold everything I own, that I have no home, no job, no wife, and no plan, and everything starts to go a little wobbly. But then I look up again, and the sun is still shining, I am not falling, there is air in my lungs, and it's just a matter of taking the next step. The tapas are good, the beer is cold, and the journey is its own reward. This is a complete paradigm-shift for me. I cannot put into words how completely funky and wonderfully weird it all is, but if you should ever sell everything, leave everyone, and strike out across an ocean to a place where you know no one, I promise you will find out.

Speaking of weird, "In-A-Gadda-Da-Vida" came on my headphones next, taking me all the way back to 1968. It was recorded in one take, drunk. A masterpiece. Was there ever an organ solo or a drum solo like that? Will there ever be another generation of artists like ours? God bless them, but Taylor Swift and Kanye West couldn't have produced that kind of genius in a thousand takes. At seventeen minutes long, by the time it was over I had relived many of the highlights of my life since 1968. Truly, truly, "what a long, strange trip it's been." You can't walk through Spain, going through all the changes I'm going through, listening to Iron Butterfly, and not see your life writ large on the road before you. Amazing.

So, the sun sets in Spain, and soon I will retire to read more Hemingway, drink a glass of tinto, and dream of life lived without a net. I thank you all for being there to catch me should I fall. God bless, and good night.

September 9

Greetings from the convent in old Leon. The sisters are thoroughly in charge and brooking no nonsense. Mass at seven, prayers afterward, and lights out at ten. The men are quartered separately from the women, so there's no risk of hanky panky (not that there ever was in a dorm of eighteen people). My only diversion is a bar that had the temerity to open across the street and that plays every song James Brown ever recorded. I have no idea why.

Another 11.58 miles today. All appendages still functioning, and otherwise "I feel good." Temperatures very cool now. Autumn and the end of this journey ever so slowly drawing nigh.

September 11

Greetings from San Justo de La Vega. After fifteen miles today and the same distance yesterday, I am roughly two-thirds of the way along, with about 150 miles to go. I'm feeling fine and am eager for Santiago.

I received an email yesterday from a writer with the link shown below to yet another story, this one published just last week in *Down East* magazine, about the final voyage of *Prodigal* in May/June of this year. The quaintness of print magazines is that the stories they tell are often overtaken by events, and the drama of the novelist who went to sea and lost his vessel but "saved his marriage" turned out to have a surprise, last act.

All along the Camino, people have asked me why and

how this could have happened, though no more than I have asked the same question myself. The truth is I don't really know. It was a plot twist out of the blue. I didn't write the script, and I didn't play the lead in the final scene. This question of why and how came up again two nights ago at dinner in Villadangos del Paramo.

Despite my efforts to escape the long arm of the law, the man seated across from me at dinner turned out to be a judge from Germany. Ordinarily nowadays I describe myself as a novelist, but not wanting to seem outgunned and thinking it might give us something to talk about, I confessed that I am a lawyer. When the usual question about how I wound up on the Camino led to the subject of my marital disaster, the next usual question of why and how my marriage ended led to the now familiar answer: "I don't know." The judge clearly was perplexed at this.

Later that day I was shaving in the bathroom with some difficulty in the waning twilight. The light switches in Spain, I have found, are never logically or conspicuously placed, and I hadn't bothered to look for one. The judge came in, immediately found the switch, and turned on the light. He grinned at me and said "lawyer," which I'm pretty sure is German for "you're not as smart as you look."

Later the next day, as I was reading the article in *Down East* and reliving those storms, something came to me like a light switched on in the darkness. Had it not been for Susan's decision three days before the storm to recommit to our marriage, I never would have given up the ship. With nowhere else to go, I would have remained aboard that leaking vessel literally come hell or high water. Knowing now the storms that were still to come farther east and north, past Newfoundland, I may well have paid for that decision with my life. This was an epiphany. Susan didn't save our marriage; she saved my life. "How could I have missed it?" I thought. God's Grace revealed. Then the image of the three year old Turkish refugee lying face down on the beach in the Mediterranean came to mind——someone far worthier of grace but for whom grace did not intervene——and the light faded again.

Life is hard, and so is faith. Much of the time we are struggling to make sense of both in the darkness. The best I can do is to make peace with the answers I may never have, to accept what I cannot understand, and to let go of what I cannot change.

September 12

Greetings from Rabanal del Camino. All is well. 15.35 miles yesterday took me through Astorgas. Later today I should pass the iron cross at the highest point on the Camino, featured in a scene in the movie, *The Way*. I have been lax about taking photos, but these are from various points in the last few days. So far all the albergues have been marvelous——clean, comfortable——and everyone very accommodating. Still seeing very few Americans but lots of Danes, Aussies, Germans, Brazilians and Italians. It's a congenial crowd, and I will surely miss the camaraderie.

September 13

Greetings from the albergue Parochial in Acebo. It is freezing cold and pouring down raining. The entire Camino I have grumbled about carrying high-tech rain

76

gear and long underwear. Not today.

The little church-run albergue is charming and run by the happiest people in Spain. Charge for a bed, hot shower, communal dinner and breakfast: zero.

Of course, getting here today cost me twelve miles of climbing on rocky ground in a cold, steady rain past the highest point on the Camino, the Cruz de Ferro (the iron cross, shown in the photos below). This is the place where pilgrims traditionally leave some symbol of their pilgrimage. There were lots of tiny memorials, stones with sayings or messages or names written on them, various mementos and pictures. I left a small steel key ring.

I have carried this key ring in my pocket for forty-one years, since I was sixteen years old. It is (now was) my oldest possession, save only a Bible given to me a year earlier. My mother bought it for me in 1974 on a day trip we made to the Naval Academy in Annapolis. It once held a key chain and medallion of the Navy mascot, both long gone. But the strong steel ring remained, and it has held every key to every house, apartment, dorm room and office, every car, boat, bike, and motorcycle, every post office box, lock, chest, drawer, desk and safe I have rented, owned or occupied in my life. I have carried it across oceans and continents, over mountains and through valleys. It was in my pocket for senior prom, on every date I have ever had, for college graduation, law school graduation, two weddings, one divorce, two births, and countless baptisms, a bar exam, a coast guard exam, some hundreds of hearings, depositions, and jury trials, and thousands of miles sailed on the open sea. It has hung from the ignitions of a '69 Buick Skylark, a '70 MGB, a '68 VW, a '72 Nova, a '79 Corolla, an '86 Volvo, an '87 Saab, a

'95 Jeep, a '97 Windstar, an '02 Miata, an '05 BMW, two Subaru Foresters, a '13 Fiat, and a '96 Ford pickup. Now, for the first time in forty-one years, I have no key to put on it. Not one. I have no house, no car, no office. There is no longer anything in my life that locks shut, which I very much hope means there is something in my life that is about to open.

September 14

Greetings from Ponferrada. Another twelve-mile hike today over rocky, beautiful terrain and through a lovely small village where I saw a sign for Casa Ramon. Isn't that the wild one from the movie, *The Way*? Couldn't stop so early, though, and had to push on.

I have been surprised that almost none of the merchants, cafes and bars take credit cards. I'm spending a total of about $33 US a day for breakfast, lunch, dinner, drinks and lodging. I'm guessing there is a large cash economy off the books, which may explain Spain's twenty-two percent unemployment. I haven't seen the platoons of idle men one would expect if unemployment were really that high, but that's just my guess. The cars here are mostly new, and I've seen very few people I would describe as poor. In fact, most folks seem to be doing well, and there is a thriving middle class. But there are many, many vacant buildings in the larger cities, so clearly not all is well with the economy.

All is well with me, however. No physical ailments to report, and the healing of heart and mind continues day by day, step by step.

September 16

Greetings from Ruitelan. It is raining buckets, and I am very happy to be warm, dry and well fed at the albergue Pequepotala with a lively group of pilgrims from Barcelona, San Sebastian, Germany, Denmark, Korea and France, all shown at the dinner table in the photos below. Another small Camino miracle is that just as my clothes were getting dirty enough to walk on their own, I stumbled into the only albergue in five days with washer and dryer service——the latter being especially rare and much needed given the weather.

Speaking of clothes, I struck up a conversation with a woman seated next to me at a cafe this morning. She turned out to be a dress designer from South Africa. She was needlessly impressed with the whole novelist thing. I told her I couldn't design a pair of shorts to save my life, and we called it even. When I expressed my disappointment that without a passport from an EU country I couldn't stay anyplace in Europe for more than ninety days, she said, "Yes, but you have an American passport, and that's golden." That really struck me. Don't believe all the naysayers. America is still admired and revered around the world.

One of the things you really appreciate on a freezing day is a good hot shower, and finding one (or one with any hot water left) has been hit or miss. I was enjoying the experience immensely this afternoon when I looked down at something on the shower floor printed in Spanish. As the words slowly came into focus, they read "Smoke this and you die." I was standing there watching my life pass before my eyes when I realized someone had used a tin of

Lucky Strike cigarettes for a soap dish. The Spanish surgeon general doesn't mince words.

All is well with me. A little wine, no cigarettes, and the end of my long journey coming clearly into view.

September 17

Greetings from the little Hobbit village of O Cebreiro, a town with a handful of thatched roof houses, a 12th century stone church, five pubs, and a single cobblestone street, perched high atop what I am told is the last mountain I'll have to climb on the Camino. I don't know what all the fear and trepidation about the climb up this mountain was for; it was a lark (for me), even in the rain, and I loved it. "For my yoke is easy, and my burden is light." Matthew 11:30.

Alas, it is not light for everyone. Today I chanced to meet again a girl from Colorado whom I mistook for a teenager when I first saw her, two weeks ago. Then, she was striding confidently past me with her arms stretched out and flapping like a goose, clearly enjoying whatever was playing on her iPod. "O to be a kid again," I thought. When I caught up to her a week later, her tail feathers were dragging. Her ankle was swollen, red and hard with tendonitis, her left knee was giving out, and she was on massive doses of Ibuprofen. Over coffee, she told me she was worried she might be doing herself some permanent damage by continuing to walk. I laughed and said, "At your age, there is no such thing as permanent damage." That's when I learned she is thirty-six, which made the fifty-seven-year-old man seated next to her feel suddenly eight-seven.

Today, my Colorado friend was moving at a snail's pace up the mountain, and the only gentlemanly thing to do was to walk beside her. This made for slow going but lots of time for conversation and stopping to admire the incredible scenery. I told her my Tale of Woe and she told me hers. She assured me I have nothing to be ashamed of to have failed twice at marriage. This cheered me, even coming from the lips of someone who looks like a child of eighteen.

At mid-morning, this woman and I stopped at a little hippie, artsy, vegetarian, tie-dyed, Zen Buddhist, goat cheese and dreadlocks cafe of the kind I have seen in surprising numbers in the mountains of Spain. The sixties are alive and well, here. She was enjoying an impossibly delicious crepe that she said she had been dreaming of for days. "The Camino provides," I heard her say to herself, and my ears perked right up.

I have experienced the mysticism of the Camino and read about it in books, but until today I hadn't heard someone mention it out loud, as a matter of fact. "Have you heard others say this?" I asked. "Oh yes," she said, as if it were common knowledge. "I'm not a religious person," she continued, "but there's definitely something weird about the Camino. It's different for every person, but everyone gets what he needs."

Just then, a young man who worked at the cafe walked by, seemed to recognize me, and welcomed me back. "But it's my first Camino," I said. "Really?" he answered. "I'm certain I've seen you here before."

Cue the Twilight Zone music. If I should fail to return from Spain, friends, rest assured that I am happily lost on the Camino in another dimension beyond space and time, enjoying crepes, scenery, and camaraderie that are truly out of this world.

September 18

Joyous greetings from Triacastela. It is a beautiful sunny day again in Spain, at last. A respectable fifteen-mile hike begun early this morning along cool, misty, high mountain ridges brought me by late afternoon into a warm, lush and verdant valley populated by the happiest dairy cows I have ever seen. A whole herd of them walked through the center of the village where I was having lunch, urged along by the farmer and a beautiful German Shepherd dog—-purebred. Enormous, regal, breed-standard German Shepherds have been in every little town I've come through for the past two days. I've never associated these dogs with farm work, but they are "shepherds" after all, so why not?

Before I leave yesterday's village of O Cebreiro behind, I want to say a word about last night's pilgrim mass. I volunteered again to do the reading in English without knowing what the selection was. I am happy to report that while reading 1 Timothy 3-13 in its entirety, my voice cracked only once (on the word "family"), and I was not incinerated at the lectern by a lightning bolt from on high. Glory Be.

Every church you pass on the Camino is an ancient treasure. Some are grand, some are plain, but all are old, and all are beloved. I have been equally impressed by the priests. Their dedication to their vocation is humbling, and their deep sense of respect for each pilgrim in turn increases each pilgrim's respect for the journey. It's hard for me to follow the mass in Spanish, so ironically the parts in Latin and Greek are the ones I know best. Last night, the priest sung the oldest prayer in the church, the *Kyrie Eleison*, as though it were the first time, and he sung a haunting, beautiful *Agnus Dei* with such reverence as if our very lives depended on those words. They do, of course.

The homily last night was spoken slowly enough that I could follow the priest's meaning in Spanish. He was talking about the spirit of the Camino and how the image of Christ appears to him in every pilgrim he meets. That suddenly explained everything for me——why people have bent over backwards to help us, treated us like royalty, and shown us such kindness. It brought to mind an old saying, and I found it today in Hebrews 13:2: "Do not neglect to show kindness to strangers, for thereby some have entertained angels unawares." The people along the Way know they can't tell the angels from the pilgrims, so they treat us all as if we are holy. I for one am hoping no one realizes how utterly mortal and earthbound I am before I reach Santiago.

Speaking of angels, I saw one today standing all alone at a fork in the Camino up ahead of me. Not seeing a sign, she was uncertain of the way to go. When she saw me she asked for guidance. Having utterly no idea but finding myself suddenly possessed by the demon of false bravado known to all men in such circumstances, I quickly and silently made the best guess I could and without missing a beat urged her confidently to "follow me."

Her name was Kasia, which is Polish for "Kathy." She was born and raised in Poland, but she lives in England near Kent——"the sunniest part." I told her I will be spending the winter in Wales——"the coldest, rainiest part."

Happily for my ego and her feet, I had chosen the right path, and an hour later it brought us to the pilgrim statue on the mountain, where we posed together for the photo below. Then the Angel of Kent flew down the Camino on long legs more beautiful than wings.

Late in the day, an older Frenchman walked up beside me and started a conversation in English—not typical for the French, I have found, so I was delighted. He is a veteran Camino hiker, he said, and he told me that while *Ah-MEHYR-i-cahns* (Americans) all think the Camino starts in St. Jean Pied du Port, it really starts in his unheard of and unpronounceable home town somewhere else in France, another five hundred kilometers away. He decided to walk the whole thing this year for the first time. When he told his wife he would be gone for three months on this journey, she said that was fine, but if he intended to leave her alone that long, she wouldn't be there when he got back. He looked at me and, speaking in the form if a question, said that for her to leave him over such a thing would be *Ahm-pah-SEE-blay* (impossible). He paused for my reaction and agreement. I wondered just how *Ahm-pah-SEE-blay* it could really be if a Frenchman were asking a strange *Ah-MEHYR-i-cahn* about the *pah-SEE-blays* in the first place.

Ever since I started the Camino, I've had Ray Charles's "Hit the Road, Jack" on my iPod. I don't know why. Maybe hearing Sweet Baby Ray sound so broken up makes me feel less broken myself. By now it's played dozens of times, and for some macabre reason I have memorized the words. Misery loves company, so in response to the Frenchman's question I had a nearly irresistible impulse to break into a bad French-accent version of the song (*Heet zee Rhode, Jacques*), but I couldn't bring myself to be so cruel. So, I told my second bold lie of the day.

"Ahm-pah-SEE-blay, of course," I said. The man walked on ahead of me shortly thereafter, satisfied. Perhaps I had been just the angel he was seeking to get through the day. I certainly hope there will be one waiting for him when he gets back to France.

September 19

Greetings from Sarria. A stunningly pretty fourteen-mile hike today. It is really so beautiful along so much of the Camino. For as old as Spain and Europe are, and as many civilizations as have come and gone here, it's amazing how open, rural, and undeveloped it all is. And the rivers . . . I still really don't get it. Even in the cities, the river water is crystal clear. Whatever they're doing, we need to be doing more of it in the USA.

I ran into a Danish girl I had met a few weeks back looking rather blue, today, sitting all alone after others had left for the next town. She was waiting for a taxi. She has done something to her knee and will not be able to finish. A real shame, now that Santiago is just sixty-six miles away. There are many such stories. I have had the luxury to take the Camino at a relaxed pace, but many are pushing themselves to complete the journey within narrow vacation schedules. It can be brutal, that way.

What follows, now, is a true story. I say this not because I am in the habit of telling false stories, but because I would scarcely believe it myself were I not there to experience it:

Today started in the ordinary way. I was the first one

awake just before five in a roomful of men in bunk beds at the municipal albergue in Sarria. This was a good morning. Sometimes I'm wide awake at 3:30. I have had trouble sleeping since I left Charleston, and when I do sleep the nights are fitful and full of dreams. This is not typical for me. I am on my third box of non-prescription sleeping pills since France. If the human body is a battery, sleep is the charger. The effect of a bad night's sleep on the body's ability to perform the next day is no different than the consequences of failing to plug in your smartphone at night: no phone and not so smart. So if I'm going to walk fifteen miles every day on these legs with a full pack, I need sleep. To make sure that happens, I take a sleeping pill every night.

But as I said, this was a good morning. I awoke rested and refreshed. When I stood up, my feet didn't hurt terrifically, and I wasn't morbidly stiff. It was going to be a good day. All the young French and Italian hotshots with their buns of steel were still sacked out, while I and my buns of Jello were greeting the dawn.

It wasn't long, though, before everyone was up and the mad rush had begun. I hate walking in great herds, so it has become my habit to linger over *cafe con leche y tostadas con mantequilla y marmalada* (coffee with milk and toast with butter and marmalade) while the masses move out. Meanwhile, I chat up perfect strangers in the corner cafe, savor the coolness of the morning air and the warmth of my coffee, read the news from America, and keep my vigil for Donald Trump to start dropping in the polls. Sometime after 8:30, when I am certain to be the last pilgrim leaving town, I shoulder my pack and head out, alone.

Only today, I wasn't alone. Where the Camino left the streets of Sarria to become a narrow goat trail through pastureland, I began to encounter pilgrims not in twos and threes but by the dozens. I remembered then what my friend and fellow pilgrim Anna Lacey-Reid had told me when she passed this way weeks ago. According to the "rules," people need to walk only the last hundred kilometers of the Camino to qualify for their Compostela——the certificate given by the church as proof of the expiation of sins granted for the pilgrimage. As a result, hordes of people begin their pilgrimage in Sarria. This changes the experience of the Camino dramatically for those who have been walking daily in solitude from France. There are now lines for every bathroom and cafe and tapas bar. Hordes of last-one-hundred-kilometer pilgrims have reserved and paid for their rooms in the albergues in every town between here and Santiago ahead of time, so pilgrims who have been walking for months are at risk of being turned away. People are louder and less gracious. The feeling of a fraternity bound by hardship and endurance has declined a bit. The Camino now has the feeling of a large group of people arriving late at mass just before the gospel and leaving right after communion.

The hucksters have shown up too, all along the Camino, seeking to fleece the hordes of late coming pilgrims with trinkets and hard-luck stories. There is a sense that the money changers have entered the temple. I passed a burro tied to a tree. A man stood nearby playing a flute. A basket was placed beside the path for donations. A sign said he was riding the burro to Santiago, which I rather doubted, looking at him and the burrow. I decided that since I was my own burro, he and his auxiliary burrow could damn well get to Santiago without my help.

Neither the crowds nor this sort of chicanery, of course, should deter anyone from walking. The way of the Camino is the way of life, with all its imperfections and frustrations. So, when I saw the crowds this morning, I plowed forward. And that's when things got weird.

As I got closer to the large group ahead of me, one walker stood out. He was a tall, thin man. Closely cropped silver hair stood out beneath a black beret. He wore a dark sport coat and long pants. He was walking in unhurried, long strides up the hill. He placed his feet carefully among the rocks on the steep path. As I got still closer, I noticed his shoes. They were not the dirty boots of a farmer or a pilgrim but ankle-high, quality-leather chukkas of the kind you might find at, say, Orvis or L.L. Bean. He was following closely behind a brown dog about the size of a collie. Coming up several yards behind this man, I noticed he carried no pack——only a gnarled, smooth wooden stick that he held through his elbows, braced against the center of his back. The stick was too short to be a cane. I imagined he must use it to control the dog, but the dog was walking obediently just ahead and needed no control. Apart from his clean and stylish boots, this man was dressed very much like a gentleman farmer, but farmers don't walk the Camino with pilgrims; they walk in their fields and tend to their livestock.

I know this man wasn't a figment of my imagination, because he was walking more slowly and deliberately than the pilgrims scrambling madly up the hill, and I watched many of them make room to walk around him. As they did so, the man continued his slow ascent of the trail, looking neither to the right nor the left, and the dog did the same.

When I caught up to this strangely dressed man on the trail, just as silently as all the rest who had passed him ahead of me, he suddenly stopped, turned around, and looked straight at me. His eyes were light in color, not brown or blue but, as best I recall, a steely gray, and intense. He had a handsome, weathered face and the closely cropped beard of a dignified, older man. He did not speak or smile; he only stared as I passed.

I smile and speak to everyone I meet on the Camino, but for some reason I do not know, I did not smile or speak to this man. I passed him as quickly as I could, and before long I was well out of sight.

The trail uphill at this point of the Camino is bordered on both sides by a steep, impassable embankment of mud, woods, briars and brambles, and beyond that are muddy fields. Everyone was following the path, and everyone followed it around an S-turn as it climbed. On the other side of this S-turn I saw, twenty yards up ahead, a tall gray-haired man in a black beret and dark sport coat with long pants, walking slowly up the trail. Our minds are wired to make sense, not nonsense, of the world around us, and I distinctly remember thinking that this was the brother—no, the twin brother—of the man I had passed. I had already moved from that thought to feelings of sentimental approval of the idea of two elderly, twin brothers, still dressing alike after all these years, on their ritual walk through the countryside, when I noticed the stick braced behind the back by the elbows, and then the dog. My mind would not accept a twin stick and a twin dog, so it moved on to the next step in its highly sophisticated neurological algorithm, which is, "Don't that beat all."

The man was still walking slowly in his clean boots and

crisp trousers, and the dog was walking at the same distance ahead of him as I passed them again. The man again turned to look at me—only me, not any of the other pilgrims who passed him before I did. This time, I could not look at him. I had a strange sense that there was something about this man I should fear—in broad daylight, with people all around me. As I passed I heard him speak, but I did not recognize the language. There was no one else near enough at the moment for him to be speaking to anyone but me, but I was afraid to answer him. He spoke again, just a few feet behind me. At any other place and time I would have turned to acknowledge someone who spoke, even if I had not understood what was spoken, but I did not. I was inexplicably, irrationally afraid. I feared this old man whom I had no reason to fear. As he spoke a third time, I hoped he might be giving some command to the dog, but when I looked at the dog, the dog was looking at me, not his master. The dog had eyes like the man's—light in color.

I was several yards ahead of the man before I stopped expecting to feel a hand on my shoulder to bring me up short for my rudeness, but there was none. I quit thinking about the man and his strange reappearance, for which I assumed there was some logical explanation. I had, after all, not been sleeping well lately. Perhaps my mind was playing tricks on me.

Later this morning, close to noon, I stopped amid the hordes crowding into a tiny bar. After waiting in line and emerging triumphantly with a beer and empanada, I was surprised to find an empty seat. The newer pilgrims were standoffish and eating by themselves. They haven't grown accustomed to the necessity born of five hundred miles to make new friends with strangers. So, I shared a table with a nice couple from South Africa. I told them about my plans to spend the winter in Wales, which they greeted with anxious smiles. "I hope you like the rain," the man said. (Is there nothing in Wales but rain?)

As I am speaking with this nice couple, a man turns to me from the next table and introduces himself—to me, only. He is Father Ben Cameron of the Fathers of Mercy, he says—an order in Kentucky. Catholic priests have made me nervous ever since my precipitous fall from grace at the end of my first marriage. Sitting there still smoldering from the wreckage of my unsanctioned second marriage, I immediately go into altar boy overdrive in order to deflect "the question": Am I a practicing Catholic. I chat him up one side and down the other about my role as a lector at the masses in Roncesvalles and O Cebreiro, about the meaningful homilies I had heard, about how devoted the priests were—even a joke about how they treated us so well only because they weren't sure who the angels were among us. He is gracious, but none of this gets a laugh or a chuckle or alters his serious and very clerical demeanor—and all the while he is talking only to me, not the two people seated next to me or the dozens of Catholics seated all around us. I find this odd. He asks me about South Carolina, and when I confuse Columbia and Greenville, I confess that I was actually raised in Baltimore, which I hope will explain why I know nothing about the Catholic cathedral in Charleston, if it comes to that.

But it doesn't. Father Cameron instead gets up to get ready to leave and resume his walk on the Camino. My beer is gone but my empanada blessedly is not, so I must remain. I breathe a sigh of relief that I will escape the encounter unscathed, with a priest of the Church actually thinking well of me. That's when Father Cameron turns and faces a patio full of people, including the other two at my table who have been listening to him all this time, and administers a blessing. To me. Only me.

There are only two rites in the Catholic church when a priest administers a blessing to one person to the exclusion of all others. One is baptism, and the other is——well, the last one. After Father Cameron's blessing I reach out to shake his hand, because I am old school enough to believe that there is power in those hands. When I do, he gives me the medal you see in the photos below. He tells me to "fear nothing," and leaves. The couple leaves then, too, and I find myself sitting there, holding the medal, and holding back my tears.

It is then that I think again for the first time since early that morning about the strange man with the dog, and my unexplained fear of him, and a sense grows inside me that I am walking not to Santiago, but to Jerusalem. Pray for me.

September 20

Greetings from Palas de Rei. All is well. I'm within spitting distance of Santiago, now. The Google map below shows the distance between here and where I started in France, although by road and not along the Camino proper. I have about forty miles to go. Should be there Thursday, but not having a map I don't really know. I have been relying on other, better prepared pilgrims for those details. I ran into one of them again, yesterday. His name is

Martin.

Martin is a bright and exceedingly polite young man of twenty-five from Slovakia. I met him at an offbeat albergue at an unscheduled stop just outside Astorgas, last week. He and I were the only two pilgrims there, so we shared dinner and a bottle of wine. Martin works for a large company as, he took care to explain, a "junior" project manager—-not yet a "senior" one, because senior project managers get a fine company-car to drive, and this is Martin's fondest dream.

Martin seemed a bit heartsick. I managed to pry out of him that he had a girlfriend back in Slovakia, a twenty-five-year old lawyer whose mother had foiled their plans to marry on the grounds that they were "too young." As he shared the details, I began to get a picture of a young woman overly involved with Mom, a mother who had unfairly judged Mathew's prospects and found him wanting, and a young man who had unknowingly just dodged a speeding bullet.

The young Spanish girl waiting on us was about Martin's age and lovely. Dark brown eyes, lips as full and deep and ready as the grapes awaiting harvest, and a long, slow, perfect curve that began just above her knees and went up miles from there, forever. Forget everything I have said about French girls. Spanish girls are softer, rounder, warmer, and not nearly so enamored with themselves. This one looked perfect for Martin, and she had been smiling a smile at us that flashed like lightning against her olive skin every time it appeared. Martin spoke no Spanish and only broken English, so I began a United Nations campaign to interest the young waitress in Martin's many fine qualities. Nothing seemed to be working. I was about to make Martin the only son of an aging billionaire Slovak oil tycoon when the obvious question occurred to me. "Tienes un novio?" (Do you have a boyfriend?)

Well, that was the end of it. Add faithfulness to the list of superlatives concerning Spanish women. But Martin and I enjoyed our dinner nonetheless. He was still asleep in our room when I left the next morning, and I frankly wondered how much farther he could bear to travel on that broken heart. Which is why I was delighted to see him a week later in Sarria in the company of two elderly women from Quebec and Norway. We all had dinner together. I called for and received their acclamation that Martin would be every mother's dream for an ideal son-in-law, which produced great blushing and a wide smile from Martin.

Yesterday on the Camino I caught up with Martin again. He invited me to be his guest in Slovakia, where he assures me all the women are beautiful and I will be given the key to the city. I have no doubt. When I asked Martin where we were headed that day, he didn't know. Having learned over that long ago bottle of wine that I was walking the Camino without a book or a map, he decided to do the same. "You are my inspiration," he said. "I am walking without a map, now." And so we walked on together, the blind leading the blind, seeing the world as we never have before.

Some of you have written to me about walking the Camino yourselves, on a tight schedule. I have carried my own pack the whole way, which slows you down and can be tough on the back and knees. There is a luggage transport service that some people use, instead. For seven

Euros, a taxi will take your pack or luggage to the next stop while you walk the same leg. No shame in that. Five hundred miles is five hundred miles no matter how you slice it.

Sarria is a large town, and lovely. As much as I like the rural areas, I love the cities along the Camino. There is nothing cheap or gauche or artificial about them. Even the newer buildings respect the architecture of centuries gone by. There is a feeling of continuity. There is nothing in the landscape that jars the senses. History is not cordoned off in parks or museums but kept alive and in use. The cities are earthy and awake with a pulse and a pace that hum the tune of the ages. It's a wondrous thing. And the pulse of Santiago de Compostela, the shrine of all of my hopes and doubts and dreams lo these many days, is so close now I can almost feel it.

September 22

Greetings from Ribadiso. 17.76 miles today, and my feet have definitely joined the revolution and are fighting for the enemy. I am now just twenty-three miles from Santiago and hope to be there Thursday midday. I am keeping up with my German friend Klaus, but it has been brutal. He has promised to arrange a bicycle tour of the Rhineland next summer for me—another gift of the Camino. Meanwhile, I am learning Norwegian folk songs, seeing my heart open to forgiveness and healing, and already missing the incredible magic of this wonderful journey, which will end too soon.

September 23

Greetings from O Pedrouzo. I am with the pilgrim hordes encamped on the outskirts of Santiago de Compostela, eagerly awaiting the invasion of the sacred city. My journey of forty days, forty nights, and nearly five hundred miles is almost complete. In the predawn darkness tomorrow, we will begin the final 12.6 mile march to the steps of the cathedral to which pilgrims by the millions have walked since the tenth century.

When I began the Camino, I carried a great burden. It was a weight made of the grievances and regrets that were piled high atop the wreckage of my marriage. Along the Way, one by one, I let go of these stones and left them by the path. Now, at the end, my burden is light. I have no one to blame, including myself, and no stone left to throw. Tomorrow, I carry into Santiago nothing but love for Susan and gratitude for you, my friends, who have been a beacon to me in the darkness. God bless you all.

September 24

Al fin, el comenzar (the end, the beginning).

CHAPTER TWO

SANTIAGO DE COMPOSTELA

When I set sail for Ireland aboard the *Prodigal* on May 25, I carried a small gift from my parish, Grace Episcopal Church of Charleston, intended for the church in Cork. It was a beautiful emblem of the cross and shield wrought by hand in stained glass by a member of Grace, entrusted to me by the vicar, carefully padded, wrapped in burlap, and tied with a string. As my ship began to founder sixteen days later off the coast of Nova Scotia, this gift was among the few items I salvaged. I later carried it with me for three days on the Wicklow Way in Ireland, intending to deliver it on foot to Cork, but that journey was interrupted so that I might begin the Camino before cold weather came to the Pyrenees in northern Spain. I have since carried this gift in my pack across emerald mountains, through crystal rivers, on the hot, dry Spanish *meseta*, and along five hundred of the most meaningful miles of my life.

This morning, I brought the gift to the steps of the cathedral in Santiago, intending to present it to one of the battalions of Spanish priests who minister to the pilgrim faithful. Imagine my surprise to meet a smiling and jovial

Irishman, Father Joe Coghlan of Cork, as the visiting celebrant of this morning's mass. As Fr. Joe reminded us in his homily, we have to pass through the vicissitudes of this life to reach the promised renewal. As all of you now know perhaps too well, I have passed through hell and high water in the course of discharging the commission given to me before that long lost voyage. I hope the people of Grace Church will suffer my errors of judgment, navigation and seamanship, at sea and on land, with the kindness and forbearance due a prodigal son. In the end, the swift, sure arrow of God found its mark, my unsteady aim notwithstanding.

Fr. Joe put us all immediately at ease, noting that pilgrims come to Santiago from all Christian traditions and that all were welcome at that table. And if that were not reassurance enough, the mass included a eulogy for an Irishman described as having two ex-wives and no great fondness for religion but an abiding love of whiskey, who died a happy man last week in Sahagun while walking the Camino. His entire, blended family appeared at mass to celebrate his life and begin their own Camino together in his memory. What an inspiration.

Of course I had to tell Fr. Coghlan that it was Michael Christopher *Hurley*—great, great grandson of a grandmother and grandfather born in Cork—who had brought this gift to him. His eyes lit up when he heard this, and he asked for the particulars of my family as if we had been gone from the Auld Sod only a short while. He mentioned that the Hurleys had a castle in Cork, and he took great pains to find paper and pencil to write down the name along with his email address. I promised to keep in touch and to find him in March, when I plan to leave

Wales and return to Ireland to lay siege to the castle and claim my inheritance. As if not a day of misfortune had passed my way since I first set sail, I have a new friend and ally in Cork and a new spring in my step on this lovely day that the Lord has made.

CHAPTER THREE

THE END OF THE EARTH

September 30

Hello all! The eternal Camino continues to the town on the Spanish *Costa da Morte* (coast of death) that Medieval Europe believed was the end ("finis") of the earth ("terre"). I left Santiago on foot Monday. I walked over a hill late today (Wednesday) and snapped this photo of my first sighting of the ocean on the Camino—a long way from where I started in France, and a long, long way from Charleston. Now it's just a quick nine-mile hike from Cece, where I am tonight, to Finisterre. I hope to arrive on Thursday.

The pilgrim walkers are down to a few crazy diehards, now. Most make the fifty-four-mile trip from Santiago to Finisterre by bus. The Swiss and Aussies are eager for the swim at the end, as if Spain in October were a tropical paradise. I will yell encouragement from shore.

All goes well with me. Thank you for your many kind messages.

October 1

I wandered into a Spanish Army recruiting center disguised as a barbershop in Santiago and got this spiffy new haircut. Should last me a year or two. In case anyone is wondering, this is how you say "just a trim" in Spanish. Before they could fit me for a uniform, I escaped on foot and headed west. A bad hairdo isn't the end of the world, but this shot definitely is. Farewell to the Camino from Finisterre.

October 2

Scenes from lovely Finesterre. I watched the sunset from these cliffs last night and half expected to see my submerged ship out on the horizon, drifting toward Spain. I dream of her still.

I was privileged to have an invitation to share not only the sunset but "dinner" sitting out on these cliffs with three women from my albergue—two South Africans and an Aussie. I was thus reminded of a lesson learned growing up around the women in my family, for whom "dinner" was a figure of speech consisting of cheese, pickled onions, fruit, chocolate, wine, and not much else. I left starving but filled to the brim with good conversation, good advice, and good company.

CHAPTER FOUR

GIFTS OF THE CAMINO: SANT POL DE MAR

Author's note: As described on pp. 29 and 30, I had the privilege of helping a fellow pilgrim one day when a leg injury left her in need of a shoulder to lean on. She responded most graciously with an invitation to spend a few days at her vacation home on the Mediterranean after my pilgrimage was finished. My time in Sant Pol De Mar, hundreds of miles to the south, seems for this reason very much a part of the Camino, for me, and one of many gifts of the journey.

Greetings from sunny Sant Pol de Mar on the Spanish Mediterranean, about an hour northeast of Barcelona. I am sitting on the shaded terrace of a cafe overlooking the water. The Med is shimmering in changing shades of blue just as F. Scott Fitzgerald described it in *Tender Is the Night*——a novel I read only four months ago with no idea that in so little time I would actually be where the feckless Dick Diver was, staring out at the same sea, wondering if I am careening toward that character's same dubious fate.

It is the off season. Almost no one who is not a local is here, and there are precious few locals. The cafe is one of only a handful still open at this time of year. The espresso machine behind the bar can be heard sputtering and expectorating the only *cafe con leche* served in hours——to an elderly couple, seated two tables away from me. Together we own the place. The old man is in a wheelchair. The years have been kinder to the old woman, and this is fortunate for both of them. The old man could not have gotten to this place without her considerable aid. He is lucky to have her, but I expect he would say that was no less true on the very first day she became his to have and to hold. They sit together, and a peace passes back and forth between them without words, like the muffled coming and going of the waves. Nothing is spoken, but much is said. It is a conversation of loud silence——the kind of silence born of understanding, acceptance, and commitment. They have endured, like Spain has endured. They are constant to each other, like the sea is constant.

But we are not alone, the elderly couple and I. Two interlopers have appeared. They are at the far end of the terrace, leaning on the railing above the beach, close to the water. They are young. She is wearing pink everything. I cannot see what he is wearing because her body is pressed against him and her head is bobbing around his, alternately administering kisses and hugs and rubbing her cheeks against his. He stands motionless while she performs this ritual with a tirelessness that calls to my mind a spider rolling up a fly. He will be done soon, I think. She is small and slight but clearly a woman. He is skinny and not much else. Between the breadth of her hips and her great shock of black hair she eclipses him. If he is not a fly, he is a bee all but immersed, head first, in this great pink flower. They surely must be in love, I decide, but it seems a love not remotely like that of the old couple. I close my eyes, partly out of politeness, but mostly because of the intoxicating serenity and bright warmth of this place.

It seems strange that only two days ago I was freezing and wet in Santiago de Compostela. I had lingered there after walking the Camino, and I lingered longer still after I returned from Finisterre. I did not want to leave. The mood was one of the final days of high school before graduation. Something familiar that I had done regularly for a long time, knew how to do, and loved——getting up and walking every day across Spain, sleeping in albergues, eating fresh bread, drinking delicious, cheap wine, commiserating with fellow pilgrims——was coming to an end. Something unfamiliar, unplanned, and unknown— the limitless blue sky or unfathomable abyss that holds the rest of my life——was beginning to open before me. I would be leaving soon. And, as Robert Frost wrote, "knowing how way leads on to way, I doubted if I should ever come back." This produced in me feelings of great tenderness for each pilgrim I met in those final days. It was for this reason that I listened attentively as one lonely old · Brit droned on about every malady he'd ever had and was going to have, and about how "the damn doctors" in Ireland are incompetent and the ones in England just keep giving him pills and bills. He is sixty-four and a lifelong bachelor. I made a point of remembering his name, and when I would ask him each day how he was feeling, the litany of medical horrors would begin anew and continue until I was the only one seated nearby who had not found means of escape. He was alone. He had no one in his life to talk to, so he talked to all who would listen for as long as they would listen.

It was this same sentimental feeling that gave me pause

when I passed a young girl lying face down on the bunk next to mine on my last night in Santiago. She was crying ever so quietly while looking at her phone. Her name was Lisa, a twenty-seven-year old from Ireland I had first met the day before when she walked into Santiago soaking wet and exhausted. Across the space between our two bunks, she had offered me chocolate that first night and told me of her Spanish boyfriend back home. When I saw tears the next day, I asked her if things had gone awry with the Spaniard. She was clearly amused at my question, and a frail laugh broke through her sniffles. She then delivered what I will remember as the winning line from my entire two months on the Camino: "A boy? Oh, no, I would never cry over a boy!"

Noting the unworthiness of my gender but still hoping to cheer her up, I changed tacks. I remembered that she was keen to see the botafumeiro at the cathedral. The evening mass was starting in half an hour. I encouraged her to go and offered to go with her. The homily, in Spanish, was about the story of Martha and Mary. In a cathedral filled to the brim with sober, dutiful Marthas, there was one smiling, young Mary from Ireland who couldn't understand a single word spoken but was there for the incense party at the end, bless her heart.

I took this young girl to dinner at Gambrinus's after mass, and like two long-lost Irish cousins we talked for hours. She told me of her large family and of the two younger brothers whose girlfriends could never pass muster with her. I asked why. "Because women are nothing but trouble." So saith the woman seated across from me.

It is now late in the evening, as I finish my tale. In Sant

Pol de Mar, today, after I left the old couple in the cafe, I began walking along the beach in the general direction of the young lovers. As I got closer, I thought of Lisa and her proverb about the dangers of women, and I wondered if I shouldn't warn the boy to "turn back now, before it's too late"——as if he would listen or could even hear me, as far gone as he was into that pink haze. But then I remembered the old couple, and their tenderness, and the old Brit, and his loneliness. It was then I knew that the young boy, like the old man in the wheelchair, had chosen the better part, and far be it from me or anyone to take it from him.

PRACTICAL ADVICE
FOR PILGRIMS

For those looking to examine their lives, their faith, their failings and their hopes while contemplating the strange amalgam of religion, culture, human courage, frailty and longing of which our world is made, there is no better place to explore those mysteries than the Camino. For many others, the Way of St. James is simply a rite of passage into young adulthood or an invigorating hike through spectacular scenery and ancient history. But by its sheer length and location, the Camino ensures that every pilgrim who walks it will know long hours and days of solitude and thoughtful introspection. Whatever you hope to find on the Camino, the mystery, mysticism, and wonder of the journey will find you.

Pilgrims approaching Santiago soon encounter others coming to the shrine of the apostle along other "caminos" from other regions, the "Camino Portugués" chief among them. In this book I have chronicled my journey along what is commonly known as the "Camino Francés," beginning in St. Jean Pied de Port in France. This is the most popular and widely used route, today, and dates back to the Middle Ages. However, for centuries people have begun the Camino from their doorsteps all over Europe, wearing down established paths from every realm.

As I write this in 2016, I have walked the entirety of the Camino Francés only once, which hardly qualifies me as an expert. I did, however, make some observations through trial and frequent error. I have distilled, here, some recommendations from my experience that may be of use to others in their own pilgrimages.

Getting There

The main airport for pilgrims arriving by air to begin the Camino Francés is in Biarritz, France. A city bus marked "Bayonne Gare" passes every few hours by the bus stop in front of the airport to take passengers to the bus and train station in Bayonne. If you did not obtain cash in the form of Euros before your trip, you will be able to do so at an ATM in the airport. Your bank debit card is the most convenient way to obtain currency. You will need cash or coins in Euros not only for the bus but for all of your expenses. As of 2015 you could count on spending about €35 per day. Take out enough money for one week at a time. Few albergues and cafes along the Camino take credit cards. ATMs are widely available, but not all of the smaller villages will have one.

Once in Bayonne you likely will encounter bunches of fellow pilgrims waiting for the bus or train to take them on the next leg to the tiny village of St. Jean Pied de Port, at the foot of the Pyrenees Mountains. St. Jean is where the Camino begins. When I arrived in Bayonne, two young girls employed as concierges in the train station very kindly directed me to the appropriate bus among several that were parked outside the station. The train is usually taken to St. Jean, but when I arrived it was out of service.

A French language phrase-book and dictionary will be helpful in the airport and the train station. While English is commonly spoken in cities like Paris, in small towns you will encounter many people in positions of authority who speak only halting English or no English at all. Soon enough on your journey, the language will switch to Spanish, and while I found Spaniards to be more commonly bilingual, the same advice applies for those pilgrims who don't have basic proficiency in the local language.

After arriving in St. Jean Pied de Port, ask for directions to the pilgrim office and go directly there. Wait until later to enjoy the wonderful cafes and restaurants on the way. There are many albergues in St. Jean, but they quickly fill up during the busy summer months. The staff at the pilgrim office keeps track of which albergues have openings and will assign you to one of them. At the pilgrim office, for a donation of a few Euros you will be given a small folding booklet known as the "pilgrim passport." This passport and the official one issued by the country of your residence are the two most important documents you will carry on the Camino. You will be asked for both at every albergue at which you stop for the night, and without them you are at risk of being turned away. Develop a system to keep them safe, on your person, and dry.

I was told that it is possible to reserve a place at some albergues online but also that this is a privilege limited to French nationals. I don't know whether that limitation truly applies (or how, for that matter, it would be enforced), but St. Jean Pied de Port is the only stop along the Camino other than Santiago itself where it may be helpful to reserve an albergue in advance, if you can. When I arrived in August, the village was in the midst of an uproarious public celebration of Basque heritage, and every room was taken. The pilgrim office on that occasion found some twenty displaced pilgrims, including myself, an empty school gym for the night. I would hope that such courtesy and concern would always prevail, but regardless, you should get about the business of finding a bed quickly upon your arrival in St. Jean and wait to explore that charming and lively town until you have done so.

Finding The Way

You will encounter most of your fellow English-speaking pilgrims at any given time with their noses deep in John Brierley's thorough and helpful guidebook to the Camino, which includes detailed maps, landmarks, and a wealth of up-to-date information on the route and the size and location of the albergues at each stop. I am a contrarian who hopes you will experience the Camino not as a hike or an expedition but as a true pilgrimage. For that reason I encourage you to leave Brierley's book—and the one now in your hands—by your armchair at home.

The Camino is well marked and well travelled. I covered the entire 530 miles of it to Finisterre without a guidebook and never got lost. You can too, by following your fellow pilgrims and, when they are not in sight, following the markers that, with few exceptions, clearly indicate the path you are to travel. These markers consist in the crudest form of yellow arrows painted or applied as stickers to fence posts, sidewalks, bridges, walls, street signs, rocks, houses, and trees. In addition to these arrows, the way has been "officially" marked by the scallop shell icon—the symbol of a pilgrim. The shells appear in various forms and shapes, sometimes cast in metal and embedded in concrete markers or sidewalks or painted on ceramic tiles mounted on the sides of buildings. For the first half of the distance between St. Jean and Santiago, the base of the shell points generally in the direction of the path. After Sahagun, a different design of shell becomes more common in which the middle striation is elongated beyond the others to "point" in the direction you are to go. The direction in which the shells are placed is generally but not always accurate, so don't follow this rule blindly.

If not with a guidebook, how can you best find your way on the Camino? The same way you find your way in life. Keep your eyes open, be wary if you have walked longer than what feels "usual" without seeing a sign you are headed in the right direction, and—most importantly—follow your fellow pilgrims. Talk to them. Consort with them. Get to know them. Stop for coffee or a beer. Introduce yourself. No one is a stranger. Everyone is from someplace else. Everyone will be happy to make your acquaintance. All of them will be happy to help and share what they know. Then, walk with them awhile and listen to their stories. Everyone is on the Camino for a reason. Be curious. If no pilgrims are nearby, ask questions of the locals. Thank them, and keep talking if they care to talk to you. Everyone, down to the smallest child in each village, knows the answer to the question, "Which way is the Camino?" They will be happy to help. They already respect and are rooting for you more than you know, because of what you have chosen to honor with your time and your effort. Get your nose out of the book and into the air. Get your eyes and ears off the page and into the moment. Experience the liberation of depending on and accepting help from others. Humble yourself. Let go. You may get lost for a little while, but you will savor the feeling of being found. Be open to the vagaries of the Way, and be amazed where it takes you.

Where to Stay

One reason so many pilgrims are busy reading a guidebook is that they have allotted themselves an unrealistic period of time—usually a month—in which to finish the entire Camino, and they are acutely concerned about traveling the "right" number of miles to get to the "right" place each day that will bring them to the end of the journey before the end of their vacation. This is lunacy. I met too many healthy young people who suffered injuries and disappointment because they were driving themselves too long and too hard every day in order to "keep up" with their friends or an arbitrary schedule. Far better to walk a part of the way in peace and comfort than to rush the entire distance under stress and in pain.

From your conversations with your fellow pilgrims each night, you will have a clear sense of where most of them are headed the next day. Sometimes, this was exactly as far as I wished to go, but more often it was a bit more of a grind than anyone would wish for. To travel the entire 530-mile length of the Camino to Finisterre in four weeks, or twenty-eight days, requires a daily average of eighteen miles. To go no farther than Santiago in the same time would take a little more than sixteen miles of walking each day. That would be a grueling pace for most adults, even without a pack to carry. However, many popular guidebooks on the Camino are designed with that kind of itinerary in mind, and the great majority of pilgrims follow that schedule.

Ten to fifteen miles per day is a far more comfortable pace and one less likely to produce injury. The irregular distance between villages means that the distance you walk each day will vary, but generally you will find an albergue at which to stay every ten to fifteen miles. You are likely to meet new groups of pilgrims each day as those racing to keep the twenty-eight-day schedule push ahead and others come up from behind. Moreover, you will be able to sleep in, relax as you enjoy a second cup of coffee at breakfast, and linger over lunch. Get started when you're ready in the morning, walk comfortably, stop often, and drop your pack when an albergue appears after you've gone about as far as you care to go that day.

The hardest single day of the Camino for most is the first one, slogging eighteen miles up the steep incline between St. Jean and Roncesvalles when they are not yet acclimated to the journey. I highly recommend stopping at the new, modern, and lovely albergue in Orrison, about six miles from St. Jean, for the first night. Ask the staff at the pilgrim office in St. Jean to reserve your room, as the albergue in Orrison is small and the only one before Roncesvalles. Not only will you appreciate an easy first day, you will savor delicious, French country cooking, served family-style on long tables in the restaurant that is part of the albergue, and spectacular views from the outdoor cafe.

What to Pack

You will be gladder of the things you *don't* bring on the Camino than the things you *do* bring. The weight of everything makes a difference when you're carrying it on your shoulders for two months and 530 miles. There are things you must have, things you may want but can do without, and things that you will absolutely never need. On these points, the conventional wisdom is not always best.

First, many guides will tell you to bring a camping mattress pad and a sleeping bag. I found that virtually all the albergues offered beds with sheets and blankets. A sleeping bag was my only bedding only once or twice, and it added needed warmth two or three times. For those occasions I recommend you bring a lightweight bag, but you are unlikely ever to spread your bag out on the floor or the ground. Leave the camp mattress behind.

It goes without saying that you need no cooking or eating utensils. All of your food and drink is purchased and eaten in albergues or cafes along the way. Besides, sampling all the variety of inexpensive pinchos and tapas and wine that northern Spain has to offer is one of the great adventures that awaits you. You will need a liter or quart-size plastic bottle to carry water, the Nalgene brand being the most common. Carry only one of these. You will be able to refill it at several stops each day, if necessary, so avoid the extra weight of carrying a second full bottle.

The usual good advice about planning and packing layers of clothing rather than large, bulky jackets applies, here. You will need a lightweight, waterproof jacket and pants. Ponchos are commonly seen, but these let in rain and wind from the sides, weigh more, tear more easily, and aren't as waterproof as high-quality rain gear from your local backpacking outfitter. Also useful is a warm, quick-drying polyester fleece jacket to wear on cool days and underneath your rain jacket for added warmth on the odd day of cold temperatures. If you are walking the Camino in winter, you'll need something more than this to stay warm, but for most who make the trip in the warm summer and fall months, a fleece jacket underneath a rain parka will offer all the warmth needed on the trail.

Lightweight pants that zip-off at the knees are sold everywhere in camping stores nowadays and are a good choice. I packed two pairs of these. Lightweight, long-sleeve, collared shirts were versatile and could be worn with sleeves rolled up or down depending on the temperature. I carried two of these. Five pairs of underpants and undershirts rounded out my kit, meaning that I needed to do laundry every four or five days. One set of long underwear tops and bottoms doubled as pajamas at night and insulation for colder days.

Boots are a constant topic of discussion among pilgrims, mostly because everyone's feet are hurting. It goes without saying that you should break them in well before the trip. You may not realize, however, how much your feet will swell on the Camino. Even if our boots are "broken in," most of us haven't walked ten to fifteen miles a day, day-in and day-out, for two months. That kind of walking will create a great deal of friction wherever your feet come in contact with the insides of your boots, most commonly at the toes. Your feet are also going to swell, making it more likely that your toes will be constricted, chafed and blistered. To avoid this, consider buying (and breaking in before you go) a pair of boots a half-size larger than what you typically wear. Pack five pairs of high-quality, well-cushioned socks—not primarily for insulation, but to protect your feet. With this outfit, you will have new underwear and socks each day for a week and new pants and shirt every two days—plenty for a pilgrim.

Everyone does laundry on the Camino. Carry a lightweight, preferably-waterproof laundry bag in your pack to segregate clean, dry clothes from dirty, rain-soaked clothes. Each albergue generally has a sink set aside for clothes washing, but these are always in high demand as pilgrims arrive in the afternoon and rush to get their laundry done and dried in the late-afternoon sun before the time comes to leave in the morning. Avoid the crowd by carrying your own lightweight, rubberized, folding bucket of the kind commonly sold at backpacking stores. Carry a small bottle of lemon scented dishwashing liquid sold by any grocery store, and use a tablespoon of it to suds up water in the bucket for the weekly wash. Refill it with fresh water for the rinse. Bring along a dozen clothes pins and a line on which to hang your clothes in the sunshine, and you'll be glad you did.

Other odds and ends of clothing and gear you will need include a good hat and sunglasses, a wristwatch, and a pair of high-quality open-toed walking sandals like those made by Teva. If (more likely *when*) you suffer blisters on your toes, it will be excruciatingly painful to slip your feet back into your boots. That's when you'll want to walk in your sandals until the blisters heal. Sandals don't provide enough lateral support and warmth to be a good choice for walking long distances daily on the Camino, but they are a much-needed option for relaxing your feet at the end of the day and for full-time use whenever you are nursing blistered toes.

You'll want to take photos of your journey, but unless you are a professional photographer, any of the smartphones sold today will offer ample quality. I took all of the photographs shown in this book with a Motorola Moto-G smartphone. You will need an adapter compatible with two-round-prong European outlets (these are the same in France and Spain but different from UK outlets) for charging your phone. Most cafes and albergues will have outlets you are welcome to use charging. Some of the newer albergues even have charging outlets and night lights above each bed.

Social media is widely used on the Camino as is WhatsApp. Virtually every restaurant, café, and albergue has free Wi-Fi available. Download the Google Translate app to your phone before you arrive, and save the French and Spanish libraries for offline use if you have space. Google takes what you speak into your phone, translates it to any language you choose, and plays the audio of the translation so you can have what amounts to a "conversation" with someone who does not speak your language. It's amazing. I used this a lot.

First aid and medical supplies deserve your careful consideration. If you are traveling from the USA, you will find that none of the usual over-the-counter medications from home are sold in Spanish pharmacies. They have never heard of Bayer aspirin, Advil, Aleve, Tylenol, Pepto-Bismol, Ny-Quill, Unisom, Ny-tol, Cort-Aid, Neosporin, Band-Aids, or just about anything you might find in a Walgreens or a Wal-Mart. They sell many of the same items, but all with unfamiliar names in Spanish. Many pharmacists didn't know what I meant by the term "moleskin," but you are sure to need yards and yards of it, so buy it in bulk. Use moleskin to eliminate friction when you feel a blister might be forming and to protect blisters and make it less painful for you to walk while they heal.

You will need a quick-drying and lightweight bath-towel for daily use. The high-wicking, synthetic backpacking towels widely sold in camping stores feel awful but are a reasonable compromise. Carrying a damp, three-pound cotton towel is not. Likewise, you will need some type of a case in which to keep whatever toiletries you require in one place so you can carry it into and out of the shower room every day. Toss in earplugs for sleeping at night.

A headlamp is a necessary tool for sorting your pack early in the morning and after "lights out," as well as for seeing the path during the occasional pre-dawn start. A digital pedometer that clips onto your belt will give you an idea of how far you've gone during the day to cheer you and keep you on pace. Pack extra batteries for each.

In addition to a lightweight internal-frame backpack (buy the smallest that will fit all your gear), you'll want a small, ultralight daypack of the kind that folds up into itself when empty. This allows you to leave your large pack in your room and carry only your valuables with you when you go walking around town at the end of the day. Bring a clear-plastic quart-size bag for keeping passports, tickets, and other documents safe, dry, and in one place.

Good luck and safe travels. For those who love lists, one with the recommended gear and supplies appears in the Appendix.

APPENDIX

Page 31:

Top: The iron cross at Atapuerca is the first of several along the Camino. The most famous, shown on pp. 43-44, is the "Cruz de Ferro" (cross of iron) at the highest point of the Camino, near the village of Manjarin.

Bottom: An image appearing on the wall of the Church of Santiago in Castrojirez with the Latin inscription, "O Mors," translated "O Death"—a reference to St. Paul's First Letter to the Corinthians, 15:55: "O Death, where is thy sting?"

Page 32:

The Shrine of San Juan de Ortego, near Agés.

Page 33:

Pilgrims make their way through Rabanal del Camino.

Page 34:

The Way.

Page 35:

Top: Yellow arrows are used as directional markers.
Middle: On the way to Castrojirez.
Bottom: Another cross located near the Cruz de Ferro.

Page 36:

Top, Middle & Bottom: Iconography on the cathedral in Burgos.

Page 37:

Pilgrims on their way into the historic section of Burgos.

Page 38:

A yellow arrow points the way.

Page 39:

The magnificent cathedral in Burgos.

Page 40:

A church building in Pamplona.

Page 41:

The main entrance doors to the cathedral in Burgos.

Page 42:

Top: Approaching Castrojirez.
Middle: Entering Castrojirez.
Bottom: Ruins of the 14th century convent of San Anton, near Castrojirez.

Page 43:

An unknown pilgrim climbs the Cruz de Ferro.

Page 44:
The author at the Cruz de Ferro.

Page 45:
Top: The tiny albergue at Manjarin.
Middle: An example of the ornamental doors common along the Camino.
Bottom: A typical dormitory style room in an albergue.

Page 46:
Another view of the ruins of the 14th century convent of San Anton, near Castrojirez.

Page 47:
Top: Fields of sunflowers are common along the Camino in the "meseta," or plains.
Middle: Often crumbling but beautiful, primitive architecture is a key attraction.
Bottom: Much of the Camino in Spain is spent walking through and alongside vineyards like this one.

Page 48:
Graffiti spotted in Estella: "Where are your dreams? Live them before dying."

Page 49:
Top & bottom: Statuary from the year 1609 in a churchyard and a street scene in Estella.

Page 50:
A street scene in Pamplona.

Page 51:
Residents of Estella attend mass at the cathedral.

Page 52:
Top & bottom: Familiar scenes along the way.
Middle: The albergue of the Virgin of Guadalupe in the town of Ciruena.

Page 53:
Top: A rock at the foot of the cross in Rabanal del Camino.
Middle & bottom: Street scenes near Ledigos.

Page 54:
Top: The Way.
Middle: The famous statues atop Mount Perdon.
Bottom: A traffic jam on the climb toward O Cebreiro.

Page 55:
Vines heavy with grapes are a common sight along the Camino in late summer and early fall.

Page 56:
Top: Stunning views of the Pyrenees Mountains can be seen on the first day of the Camino, heading to Orrison.
Middle: The author shown beside a gigantic statue of a pilgrim atop a mountain not far beyond O Cebreiro.
Bottom: Pamplona street scene.

Page 57:
Medieval pilgrims brought back shells from the sea to prove to others they made the entire journey to Finisterre. The shell became a symbol of the Camino, and pilgrims

like this one wear them from their packs, today.

Page 58:
The author poses with a statue of a pilgrim drinking from a gourde beside a water fountain near Rabanal del Camino.

Page 59:
Top & bottom: The way and the sign.

Page 60:
Ancient statuary near Puente La Reina.

Page 61:
Pilgrims newly arrived in St. Jean Pied de Port make their way among Basque holiday partiers.

Page 62:
Ancient statuary near Puente La Reina.

Page 63:
An 11th century baptismal font that was in service at the tiny church in O Cebreiro when Saint Francis of Assisi came through town on his pilgrimage to Santiago.

Page 64:
A government office building in Pamplona.

Page 65:
Top: The stone cross at Rabanal del Camino.
Middle: The author in the Pyrenees just inside the Spanish border, near Roncesvalles, next to a stone marker that reads, "765 kilometers to Santiago."

Bottom: Iconography on the outside of the cathedral in St. Jean Pied de Port.

Pages 66-67:
Scenes from Finisterre.

PACKING LIST

__ Zip trousers (2)	__ Sunblock	__ Euro plug adapter
__ LS Shirts (2)	__ Folding bucket	__ Earplugs
__ Underpants (5)	__ Clothes pins	__ Nail clippers
__ Undershirts (5)	__ Clothesline	__ Zip-lok bag
__ Socks (5)	__ Dishwash liquid	__ Surgical scissors
__ Fleece jacket	__ Laundry bag	__ _____
__ Sandals	__ Smartphone	__ _____
__ Rain gear	__ Phone charger	__ _____
__ Sun hat	__ Headlamp	__ _____
__ Sunglasses	__ Spare batteries	__ _____
__ Pajamas	__ Pedometer	__ _____
__ Backpacker towel	__ Notepad & pen	__ _____
__ Toiletries in case	__ Passport	__ _____
__ Medicines	__ Sleeping bag	__ _____
__ Moleskin (10 yds)	__ Hiking boots	__ _____
__ Band-aids (100+)	__ Backpack	__ _____
__ Neosporin	__ Daypack	__ _____
__ Alcohol wipes	__ Swimsuit	__ _____
__ Surgical tape	__ Water bottle	__ _____
__ Gauze pads	__ Washcloth	__ _____
__ Talcum powder	__ Spare glasses	__ _____

ABOUT THE AUTHOR

Michael Hurley is an American author of three novels and numerous works of nonfiction. His debut novel, *The Prodigal,* won the Chanticleer Reviews Grand Prize. It was described as an "artistic masterpiece" by *Foreword Reviews* and as one of the top five novels of 2013 in *Booktrib.* His second novel, *The Vineyard,* won the 2015 Eric Hoffer Award for General Fiction and was described as "deliriously satisfying" by *Kirkus Reviews.* An essay collection, *Letters from the Woods,* was shortlisted for Book of the Year in 2005 by *ForeWord Reviews.* His third novel, *The Passage,* was completed during the six months he spent living in England and Wales after finishing the Camino. He set sail from Calais, France on May 5, 2016 bound for La Palma, in the Canary Islands, on a voyage around the world aboard his 1967 sloop, *Nevermore.* He keeps a journal and stays in touch with readers on his website, www.mchurley.com.

Lightning Source UK Ltd.
Milton Keynes UK
UKOW06f0810301016

286460UK00009B/160/P